PATH TO THE PACIFIC
THE STORY OF SACAGAWEA

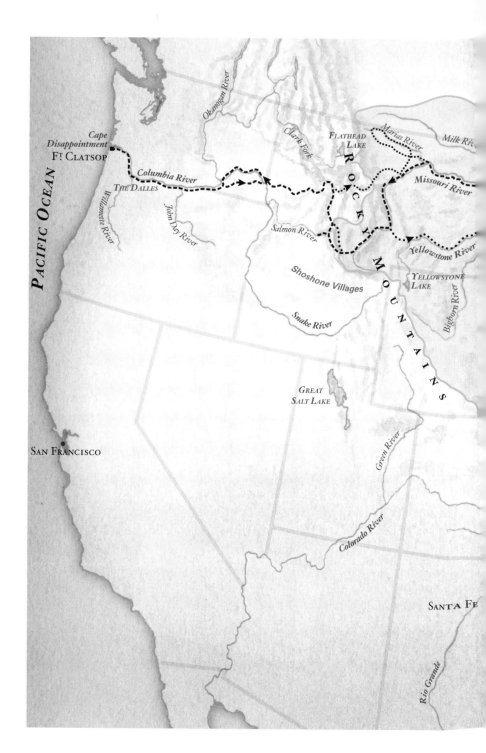

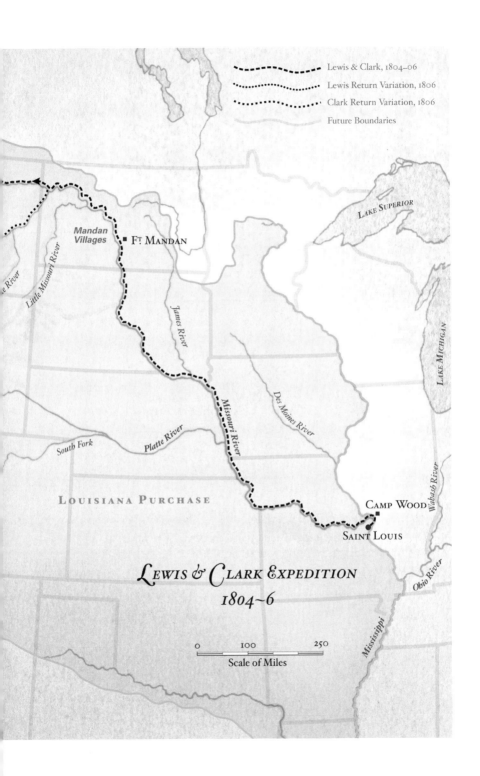

Lewis & Clark, 1804–06
Lewis Return Variation, 1806
Clark Return Variation, 1806
Future Boundaries

LAKE SUPERIOR

LAKE MICHIGAN

Mandan
Villages   ■ F⊤ MANDAN

Little Missouri River

James River

Des Moines River

Missouri River

South Fork   Platte River

Wabash River

LOUISIANA PURCHASE

CAMP WOOD
SAINT LOUIS

Obio River

LEWIS & CLARK EXPEDITION
1804–6

Mississippi

0   100   250
Scale of Miles

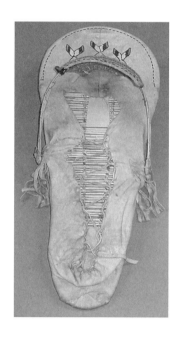

Shoshone or Paiute cradleboard of the type that Sacagawea might have used for her baby, Jean Baptiste

PATH TO THE PACIFIC
THE STORY OF SACAGAWEA

by NETA LOHNES FRAZIER

STERLING PUBLISHING CO., INC.

New York

A FLYING POINT PRESS BOOK

Design: PlutoMedia
Front cover art: Mark Hess for the United States Postal Service
Frontispiece: Courtesy of the Northeastern Nevada Museum
and Historical Society.

Library of Congress Cataloging-in-Publication Data

Frazier, Neta Lohnes, 1890-
Path to the Pacific : the story of Sacagawea / Neta Lohnes Frazier.
p. cm. -- (Sterling point book)
"A Flying Point Press book"--T.p. verso.
Updated ed. of: Sacagawea : the girl nobody knows. 1967.
Includes bibliographical references and index.
ISBN-13: 978-1-4027-4518-8 (trade)
ISBN-10: 1-4027-4518-4
ISBN-13: 978-1-4027-4138-8 (pbk.)
ISBN-10: 1-4027-4138-3
1. Sacagawea--Juvenile literature. 2. Shoshoni women--Biography--Juvenile literature.
3. Shoshoni Indians--Biography--Juvenile literature. 4. Lewis and Clark Expedition (1804-
1806)--Juvenile literature. 5. West (U.S.)--Discovery and exploration--Juvenile literature.
I. Frazier, Neta Lohnes, 1890- Sacagawea. II. Title.

F592.7.S123F739 2007
970.004′97--dc22
[B]

2006032146

2 4 6 8 10 9 7 5 3 1

Published by Sterling Publishing Co., Inc.
387 Park Avenue South, New York, NY 10016
Original edition published by David McKay Company, Inc., NY
under the title *Sacagawea: The Girl Nobody Knows*
Copyright © 1967 by Neta L. Frazier
New material in this updated edition
Copyright © 2007 by Flying Point Press
Map copyright © by Richard Thompson, Creative Freelancers, Inc.
Distributed in Canada by Sterling Publishing
c/o Canadian Manda Group, 165 Dufferin Street
Toronto, Ontario, Canada M6K 3H6
Distributed in the United Kingdom by GMC Distribution Services
Castle Place, 166 High Street, Lewes, East Sussex, England BN7 1XU
Distributed in Australia by Capricorn Link (Australia) Pty. Ltd.
P.O. Box 704, Windsor, NSW 2756, Australia

Printed in China
All rights reserved

Sterling ISBN-13: 978-1-4027-4138-8
ISBN-10: 1-4027-4138-3

For information about custom editions, special sales, premium and
corporate purchases, please contact Sterling Special Sales Department
at 800-805-5489 or specialsales@sterlingpub.com.

To my Sister
Ruth Lohnes Rutledge

CONTENTS

PATH TO THE PACIFIC
THE STORY OF SACAGAWEA

PART ONE

THE PREPARATION

THE YEAR IS 1789.

In New York City, on April 30, General George Washington, age fifty-seven, stands on the balcony of Federal Hall, Wall Street, and takes the oath of office as first President of the United States.

In Paris, Thomas Jefferson, forty-six years old, completes five years of service as Minister to France and starts home to accept the assignment as Secretary of State in Washington's cabinet.

In Valence, France, twenty-year-old Napoleon Bonaparte, a Corsican, graduates from military school and becomes a second lieutenant in an artillery regiment.

In Albemarle County, Virginia, Meriwether Lewis, age fifteen, son of a wealthy plantation owner, grinds away at Latin, mathematics, and science under a private tutor, preparing to enter William and Mary College.

In frontier Kentucky, near the falls of the Ohio River, red-headed William Clark, nineteen years old, leaves his home at Mulberry Hill and goes off to join the Army.

And far to the west, somewhere near the border of the future states of Idaho and Montana, an area so remote it has never yet been seen by a white man, a Shoshone Indian mother holds to her breast the newborn baby girl who will one day be called Sacagawea.

Six persons, except for Washington and Jefferson as unrelated as human beings could be. Their chances of ever being drawn together in any significant way, only a computer could estimate. Even a computer might balk at the possibility that the Indian baby will become the heroine in one of the greatest dramas of American history and that she will be, for a few ticklish moments, the pivot on which the future of that history will swing.

The threads of which the drama is to be woven run slowly from the spindle of time.

George Washington passes from the scene in 1799, bestowing his role on the young country he has helped to create. He has nursed it through its infancy until now it stands upon sturdy legs and begins to move out beyond the Alleghenies.

Thomas Jefferson expounds his political philosophy so effectively that in 1801 he becomes third President of the United States.

Napoleon Bonaparte mounts through a military career to the exalted position of Emperor of France.

Meriwether Lewis forsakes his planned college course to join the Army and skirmish through Kentucky and Ohio.

William Clark, already in the Army, meets Lewis and becomes his closest friend.

As for the Indian baby, from birth she is being trained by nature and circumstances for the great moment in her future. That this is true is revealed by her childhood name, Bo-i-naiv, meaning Grass Woman. White people who hear it later on form a mental image of it as "Bowie Knife" and so pronounce and spell it.

Since the childhood names of Indians often reflect characteristics or unusual circumstances and change from time to time, there may well be something about this child's reaction to life which gives her the name, Grass Woman.

Her people, the Shoshones, are at this time very poor and greatly diminished in numbers through battles with their enemies, the Plains Indians. The latter have acquired guns and ammunition from traders along the Mississippi and lower Missouri rivers. They have thus been able to defeat the Shoshones, who have only bows and arrows. Steadily the latter have been driven farther and farther back into the refuge of the Rocky Mountains.

For generations the Shoshones have been horse Indians. They know little of canoe travel, their streams being too swift, shallow, and turbulent. Because they own large herds of horses and mules, their only wealth, and because they must rely on natural feed for them, they can never remain in one place for more than a few days, but must constantly be on the move in search of grass.

"Grass" may very well be the first word little Bo-i-naiv learns, and she says it whenever she sees her mother and older sisters begin to take down the leather tepee which they call home. Already she knows that grass, and consequently moving, are the great facts of their lives. She feels perfectly natural in this manner of living. To remain in one place more than a few days seems to her strange and tiresome.

She is also well accustomed to the scant, irregular food of nomadic people, especially in mountain country. In the spring and early summer, when the salmon come up the rivers from the Pacific Ocean to spawn, the Shoshones gorge themselves on their rich pink meat. After the salmon are gone they depend on chance deer, elk, and game birds. If these are not available, the Indians must get along on berries and many kinds of roots which plains people do not know.

Thus, by long custom, Bo-i-naiv is able to exist and remain healthy on an ever-changing diet and knows how to find food in seemingly barren country. This, also, is preparation for the time to come.

As she grows older, she makes friends among the girls of her tribe. One is Otter Woman, a few years older than herself. Where does this girl get her name? Is she sleek and beautiful like the little water animal? Or is it, rather, from a deformity of her legs that makes her, like the otter on land, slow-moving and awkward, though sweet and gentle of disposition? If so, she is not alone in this handicap. Many Shoshones have crooked legs, perhaps because they ride horseback so much, but more likely because of their poor diet. Otter Woman perhaps gets her name because she is a little more noticeable in her defect than other girls.

Another friend of Bo-i-naiv is Leaping-Fish Woman. Here the meaning comes clear. This little girl is as lively and active as a fish in water. She is impulsive and quick to act. She and Bo-i-naiv make a good pair, with Otter Woman, the older and slower one, to watch over them.

The homeland of the Shoshones is that beautiful, harsh, perpendicular country along the Continental Divide where Idaho and Montana meet. In the summer they live on the

Idaho side, along the Lemhi and Salmon rivers. Toward fall, when the salmon disappear and game grows scarce, they move eastward across the Bitterroot Mountains to the area of the Three Forks of the Missouri River. Occasionally buffalo come up the river this far and may be killed with bows and arrows. Failing in this, the Shoshone braves make quick dashes into the plains to secure the meat and buffalo robes they need for the bitter winters.

On one such occasion, in the fall of 1800, they camp near the Three Forks. While the men prepare for the hunt, the women scatter to pick berries which they will dry and mix with pounded buffalo meat to make pemmican. This is a nutritious food on which they can sustain life during the time of deep snows and scarcity of game.

Suddenly they are surprised by a band of Gros Ventres or Hidatsas and Minnetarees from the plains. The Shoshones run in all directions, seeking refuge in clumps of bushes, since this is treeless country. Some escape, and some are killed. Eleven-year-old Grass Woman tries to ford a stream to the safety of the undergrowth on the other side. A Minnetaree brave plunges into the water on his horse and snatches her up in front of him. She bites and scratches, but he only laughs and holds her more tightly. He likes her spirit and tells her he will bring her up as his own daughter.

At the camp of the victors, Bo-i-naiv is somewhat comforted to find eight other children, four boys and four more girls. Among them are her friends, Otter Woman and Leaping-Fish Woman. The children have their own small cooking fire to which food is brought by their captors. They are sad and do not want to eat. They think and talk only of escape.

The Minnetarees move across country to bypass the great falls of the Missouri, then follow it eastward toward their headquarters in what will be North Dakota. Elk Horn, the oldest of the stolen children and their leader, urges them to pretend they have forgotten their own people so that their captors will relax their watchfulness. Then, when an opportunity offers, they may more easily get away.

They do as he suggests, and at last their chance comes. One night the Indians camp near the river where much driftwood has gathered. The young captives bring in some of this wood for the evening fires. Elk Horn sees several logs and conceives the idea of rolling one into the river. By clinging to it, he thinks, the children can float across the stream, then start back toward home. He plans to steal a bow and arrows with which they can secure food on the way.

Following his instructions, the children pretend to settle down for the night, waiting for their captors to do likewise. However, on this night the Indians sit long about their fires, most of the children fall asleep. Only Elk Horn and Bo-i-naiv manage to keep awake. Hours pass before the camp becomes quiet. Then Bo-i-naiv sees Elk Horn crawl slowly from the group toward the nearest of the sleeping braves. Minutes later he backs away with the precious bow and arrows he has managed to take without wakening their owner. As he starts toward the river, he signals her to rouse the other children.

She crawls from one to another. Beside each, she places her hand over the sleeper's mouth while she whispers in his ear, "Wake up! It is time to go!"

One by one the children rouse from sleep and slip away into the darkness. Now only two are left, Leaping-Fish Woman and Otter Woman. Bo-i-naiv tries one, then the other, but cannot waken them. She can get away herself, but she will not leave these two so dear to her. Already, at eleven, she is loyal to the point of danger or even death.

Becoming desperate, she forgets to be careful. She pulls harder at Otter Woman's arm. The older girl jumps and shrieks, fearful that one of her captors has seized her. Her cries rouse the whole camp, and the Indians discover the disappearance of the children. In the darkness they cannot find them, but they do not worry. Six children cannot go far before morning. They content themselves with moving the three girls up into the main camp where they can be watched more closely.

The six children who escaped are never found. Soon their captors give up hunting for them. Disheartened, the three girls keep to themselves, each day moving farther and farther from home. Leaping-Fish Woman talks constantly of making another attempt to get away, but Otter Woman, knowing her own awkwardness, is afraid to risk it.

Perhaps Bo-i-naiv remembers how hungry she often was in the mountains, while here on the plains there is always plenty of good food. Perhaps she remembers her father, lying dead after the attack, and thinks her brothers may have met a like fate. If that should be true, going home can mean nothing to her except slavery or to be taken at once as the wife of the ugly, middle-aged man to whom her father betrothed her when she was little more than a baby. In payment, he received three good horses, as much as a fine mule would cost. If she goes back to her people, her future husband can claim her any time he chooses.

There is another reason why she prefers not to go back. She is still Grass Woman, who loves to be on the move. She does not want to settle down as a wife. Her captors have treated her kindly, and she does not fear them any more. She is learning their language and longs to see for herself the places and people of whom they talk. With an ability for decision rare in one so young, she closes the door on her past and looks toward a new and better future. When Leaping-Fish Woman sets a day for leaving and asks her to go, she chooses rather to remain with Otter Woman. She does not guess that she is thus taking one more step toward the great moment when she will become part of history.

Slowly but inexorably the drama begins to unfold.

The new country of George Washington moves steadily westward.

President Jefferson asks Meriwether Lewis to become his private secretary.

Napoleon, having acquired Louisiana from Spain, thinks of selling it to finance his wars.

Lewis learns of the President's interest in the country beyond the Mississippi and begs for the chance to explore it.

Clark, though without formal schooling, studies geography and map-making, in which he becomes an expert.

In the homeland of their captors, beside the Missouri River, Grass Woman and Otter Woman cling together, but are not actually unhappy. Their owner, who calls them his slaves, treats them the same as his daughters. They have plenty to eat, and though they work hard, it is what they have always been accustomed to. Grass Woman learns to speak the Minnetaree language and can interpret for Otter Woman what their captors say.

For the first time, the two girls see white men. They have heard that such beings exist, but have never before seen one. These men are traders from the Hudson's Bay and North West

Companies who buy furs from the Indians in return for blankets, beads, copper and brass kettles, red and blue cotton cloth and, most prized of all, guns, powder, and bullets. Some of these traders take Indian wives. The girls of the tribe think it very fine to have a white husband, but the owner of the two Shoshone slaves refuses all offers for them. He says they are not yet old enough to become wives.

One day a black-haired French trader comes to the camp. His name is Toussaint Charbonneau. The Indians know him because he has visited them before. Though he earns his living by trading with them, he despises them and will not trouble himself to learn their language beyond the few words needed to buy and sell.

He has, however, adopted many of the Indian ways, among them a love of gambling. He often joins in the Indian games and sometimes wins horses or furs. Now he gambles for bigger stakes, the two Shoshone girls, and wins.

Aghast at what he has done, their former owner offers to stake everything he possesses against the girls, but the Frenchman refuses to play any more. He has won two strong young slaves and will not risk losing them.

The frightened girls can do nothing but obey their new master, who takes them still farther east to the Mandan country where he has a wife of that tribe. She is a kind, gentle woman, but her health is poor, and she cannot do all the work

Charbonneau puts upon her. She welcomes the assistance of the two girls. Under her teaching they learn to tan skins of deer and buffalo, to make clothing and moccasins, and to plant, water, and harvest the crops of beans, corn, and squash the Mandans raise in the fertile river valley. They also learn how to cure many diseases by the use of herbs, roots, and bark of trees.

In the cellar-like lodge, made of logs set upright, partially sunken into the ground and roofed over with branches and sod, the two girls find warmth and comfort they have never before known. The Mandans do not roam about like the Shoshones. There is permanence in their living, which pleases Otter Woman, with her gentle, domestic disposition and physical handicap.

Bo-i-naiv, who loves the constant moving she has known in the mountains, is not so easily tamed. No doubt she annoys Charbonneau, who is more than forty years old and wants nothing but peace and comfort when he comes home. When he is tired and hungry, he sometimes becomes violently angry and beats the girls. Otter Woman accepts it as the lot of womankind, but Bo-i-naiv probably talks back and makes him still more angry.

Old for her years, she understands that Charbonneau is yet a child in many ways, that beneath all his boasting, bragging and scolding, he is timid and easily alarmed by any emergency. He is proud of being a full-blooded Frenchman, not a half-breed like many of the fur traders he knows. So he is vain and selfish, fretful and irritable. Bo-i-naiv is forced to obey him, but she does not like him.

It is during this time of her life that Bo-i-naiv becomes Sacagawea, or Bird Woman. Who gives her this name, and why? Long after her death, some historians will argue that it is a Shoshone name meaning, "She who pulls (pushes, launches) boats (canoes)." Hardly likely, when her people do not use canoes.

"Oh, but they do not give her the name in her childhood," say those who hold this view. "It is awarded to her years later when they see her come up the great river with the white chiefs, Lewis and Clark. These men do have boats and must pull them laboriously through rapids and over sandbars by means of tow lines."

An intriguing idea, until one reflects that the girl's name appears in the journals of the two captains and one of their sergeants months before this.

More probable is it that she receives her new name, Tsa-ka-ka-wea, or Bird Woman, from the Hidatsas, a tribe related to the Gros Ventres and Mandans, who live with them. They call her Bird Woman for the same reason that modern American parents and relatives give children endearing nicknames such as Skippy or Toad, Little Shortcake or Pickle. Something about her reminds them of a bird.

Perhaps she hops lightly through the woods as she gathers twigs and branches for the supper fire. Perhaps she is fond of birds and saves scraps of food for them. Perhaps she sings at her work, since Indians do delight in song. For whatever reason, the people around this child find her spritely and charming, so they give her a lovely name.

When Captain Meriwether Lewis first hears it, the guttural sounds in which these people speak lead him to write the name "Sah-cah-gar-wea," with a hard *g* sound in the middle. But Americans do not take readily to sounds coming from deep in the throat. Captain Clark solves the problem by calling the girl Janey.

Perhaps it is he who is responsible for the remembered *j* sound years afterward when his journal is being edited with the help of young George Shannon, a member of his party. Shannon recalls the *j* of Janey and spells the name "Sacajawea." This spelling will come into common use, though in time the Bureau of American Ethnology will assert that it should be "Sacagawea," with the hard *g*. Areas of North Dakota will continue to insist that the name is "Sakakawea," or "Tsakakawea." Technically, one or the other of these is probably right, but it will be a practical impossibility to change the form generally accepted throughout the West. Who will chip all the *j*'s off the granite monuments and substitute *g*'s or *k*'s? Who will do over the lettering on all the historical markers and the names on bridges, schools, and parks? Who will replace all the neon signs on hotels and motels and correct the millions of highway and other maps?

Of all this controversy which is to come, the young Indian girl is, of course, totally unaware as she goes about her work among her Mandan and Hidatsa friends. She is now fifteen years old, according to legend rather small and pretty in her own Indian way. Again it is legend, unprovable but quite probable, that says a handsome Mandan youth begins to notice her. As she hoes the corn, he talks to her. Soon they fall in love. He vows to buy her from her owner. If need be, he will pay as many as ten horses. Laughing and confident, they go to Charbonneau with their plans.

The Frenchman is outraged. Where before he has thought of the two girls as children and slaves, he now sees they have become desirable young women. Jealousy flares up in him. He drives the youth away and sets his Mandan wife to watch Bird Woman whenever she leaves the lodge.

The older woman is sympathetic. She turns the other way when the boy creeps into the cornfield to talk to the sorrowing girl. He promises her he will go off to war and win many trophies. When he returns, not even the haughty Frenchman can refuse him.

Their dream is not to be realized. Word comes that the handsome youth has been killed in battle. Like girls the world over, Sacagawea weeps for her lost love until she learns that people do not like a weeping woman. She learns to hide her grief behind a blank face, but she begins to hate Charbonneau. Perhaps she lets him see it. Perhaps this is the reason for the story that he likes Otter Woman the better of the two.

About this time, the Mandan wife dies, but Charbonneau shows no feeling. He has two pretty girls to think about.

The threads of the drama begin to interweave.

The new republic, growing daily in strength and ambition, as George Washington dreamed, finds its use of the Mississippi River blocked by France. A commission goes to Paris, hoping to buy the port of New Orleans so the river may again be open for traffic.

Napoleon, desperate for money, sells the whole of Louisiana to the United States for eleven and one-quarter million dollars.

President Jefferson gains the consent of Congress to send Meriwether Lewis on an expedition to explore the new territory and cross the Rocky Mountains to the Pacific Ocean.

Lewis chooses William Clark as his co-captain and companion.

First Otter Woman, then Sacagawea, is taken as a wife by Charbonneau. He has adopted as his own the Indian custom of multiple wives. Otter Woman presents him with a son whom he names for himself, Toussaint, Junior.

This child is not mentioned in the journals of Lewis and Clark or anywhere else until years later when he lives in St. Louis and attends school at the expense of William Clark. Because nothing is written of him, some people will deny that he exists.

But consider the man, Toussaint Charbonneau. Consider his pride in being a full-blooded Frenchman. Charbonneau is an honored name in the part of French Canada where he was born, and Toussaint is often chosen to go with it. Is it likely that he will not pass on the proud name to his firstborn son? If the name has not already been used, will he not give it to Sacagawea's son, born two or three years later, instead of the next-favored name, Jean Baptiste?

Though Charbonneau has traded for many years, he has never learned to speak English. When he wishes to talk with the traders of the Hudson's Bay or North West Company he must do it through an interpreter. Fortunately for him, another Frenchman lives in the Mandan villages, a man named René Jusseaume. He speaks English acceptably, having learned it from the great Canadian explorer, David Thompson, whom he accompanied on some of his journeys. Jusseaume has now been living among the Mandans for more than ten years and has a Mandan wife and a family of children. With no doctor about, he has learned to take charge himself when his wife gives birth to one of their offspring. Before long, his experience will come in handy.

At last the plot of the great drama begins to move.

Lewis and Clark scour the western country for men qualified to join their expedition. They want unmarried men who will not be looking back with longing to wives and families. They must have men with many different abilities: a carpenter to build their winter fort, a blacksmith to keep their guns in order, capable boatmen to fashion and operate canoes and pirogues, hunters of unusual skill, since they must live off the land through which they will travel. Most important of all, they will need interpreters to enable them to communicate with the many Indian tribes. The first one they employ is George Drouillard (Drewyer), part French and part Indian. He is an expert in the universal sign language by which Indians of all tribes exchange basic information.

Lewis has a large keelboat built to his own specifications. When it is ready, he sails down the Ohio and up the Mississippi to St. Louis. There he joins Clark in the early fall of 1803.

With the men they have chosen, they set up a winter camp and prepare to begin the journey up the Missouri the following spring.

Clark, at thirty-three, is the oldest of the crew; George Shannon, sixteen, the youngest. Clark trains the men, while Lewis spends most of his time assembling supplies. These he has packed in bales, each containing some of all the different items. Then, if one bale should be lost or spoiled, it will not mean the loss of the entire supply of any one kind of goods.

He buys many yards of oilcloth for wrappings to keep out dampness and mold. Large sheets of this material will be used to cover the canoes and at times will serve as makeshift tents. They carry quantities of simple medicines and fourteen bales of presents for the Indians. Among these are beads, red, white and blue, imported from Italy for the fur trade. Lewis has heard that Indians prefer blue beads, but he underestimates this preference. Later on, he will wish he had brought many more.

He urges all of his men who can and will to keep journals or diaries of daily events. He senses that this expedition will be important in the history of the United States and that every possible record of it should be made. A number of his men cannot read or write, but four sergeants and three privates keep records of all or part of the journey.

The keelboat is fifty-five feet long and draws three feet of water. For propulsion it carries a large, square sail and twenty-two oars. Besides this boat, there are two pirogues or oversize canoes. The larger one is painted white and has seven oars; the smaller, red, with six oars. The keelboat is armed with a swivel gun which fires indifferently but makes an impressive roar.

The captains take a few extra men on this first leg of their journey. They know they will have to spend a winter somewhere on the Missouri and from that point plan to send back the keelboat with Lewis's reports and specimens of animal and plant life for President Jefferson. The preliminary journey will also give Lewis a chance to try out his men and choose the most able for the final dash to the Pacific.

Like others of his time, he knows practically nothing about the country west of the Mississippi River. He still clings to the dream of a water route across the continent, which dates back to Christopher Columbus. He believes he and his party can navigate the Missouri to its source, then with a short portage of perhaps twenty miles, one full day's overland journey, set their boats down again in the Columbia River and sail to the Pacific.

On May 14, 1804, the expedition leaves St. Louis. Clark captains the flotilla while Lewis rides along the shore on one of the two horses provided for the hunters. He has with him his big black Newfoundland dog, Scammon. Clark's personal companion is his Negro servant, York, a cheerful giant of a man who was given to Clark by his father years before. The two have grown up together and are more like brothers than master and slave. York can speak French after a fashion and sometimes serves as interpreter, since neither Lewis nor Clark has learned this language.

Through the long, hot summer of 1804 the men toil up the Missouri for sixteen hundred miles. Sometimes the midday heat is so intense that even Scammon suffers sunstroke and has to be carried to a creek for relief. The men meet many tribes of Indians, some determined not to let them pass without paying heavy tribute. Both captains show their ability to handle crises. Before the end of the summer, they have established in the minds of all the Missouri tribes respect for the new Government in Washington.

A few of the men rebel against the hard work and strict discipline. Captain Lewis is ruthless in the face of insubordination. The rebels are flogged, and two are dismissed.

In October the weather turns very cold. Snow begins to fall. The captains decide it is time to stop for the winter. They choose a place about three miles below the villages of the Mandan Indians, who are friendly and more intelligent than others they have met.

In a grove of cottonwood, elm, and ash trees, they build Fort

Mandan, near the site of the future city of Bismarck, North Dakota. Sergeant Patrick Gass, under date of September 3, 1804, tells of its construction:

> *The huts were in two rows, containing four rooms, each fourteen feet square and joined at one end forming an angle. When raised about 7 feet high a floor of puncheons of split plank were laid, and covered with grass and clay; which made a warm loft. The upper part projected a foot over and the roofs were made shed fashion, rising from the inner side, and making the outer wall about 18 feet high. The part not enclosed by huts we intend to picket. In the angle formed by the two rows of huts we built two rooms, for holding our provisions and stores.*

The captains soon have a good high stockade wall built across the open side of the triangle with a heavy gate which can be bolted to keep out unwanted visitors.

Among the first to come is the French trader, René Jusseaume, who is at once employed as interpreter to the Mandans. He is given the hut next to that of the captains and moves in with his wife and children. Soon thereafter, Toussaint Charbonneau returns from a trading trip and likewise seeks work as an interpreter, but to Indians a little farther up the river, especially the Minnetarees. Learning of the captains' plan to ascend the Missouri to its source, he tells them he has two wives of the Shoshone tribe. These people inhabit the Rocky Mountains and have many horses. The two women, he says, can interpret for the white men when they wish to buy animals to carry their goods over the mountain portage. Lewis asks to see the women.

Charbonneau brings Otter Woman and Sacagawea to call. Neither of them understands English, so the captains cannot talk with them. They take note that Otter Woman has a young child and is expecting another. Sacagawea also is obviously to become a mother in a short time. They do not fancy the idea of taking a baby on their journey. Perhaps during the winter they will find a man who can interpret Shoshone. For the time being, they employ Charbonneau as interpreter for the Minnetarees who swarm about the post. They allow him to move his family into the hut with the other interpreter.

Before long they discover that Charbonneau cannot even understand Minnetaree without Sacagawea's help. He has to pass it on to Jusseaume in French. The latter turns it into English for the captains. They begin to think more favorably of taking the girl with them.

From the first, Captain Lewis has a poor opinion of Charbonneau. After the expedition he will write of him:

A man of no peculiar merit, was useful as an interpreter only, in which capacity he discharged his duties with good

*faith, from the moment of our departure from the Mandans
. . . until our return.*

Charbonneau feels Lewis's disdain. He becomes sulky and announces that if he does go on the expedition he will do no ordinary work and will be free to return home any time he chooses to do so.

Lewis shrewdly sizes up his man. He needs the young wife and cannot have her without taking her husband also. Yet he cannot afford to let any man dictate terms. He therefore takes the chance and cancels his agreement with the Frenchman.

Sacagawea and Otter Woman understand only that their man has angered the white chiefs. They both have built up their hope of a reunion with their own people, and now it is gone. Probably they scold Charbonneau, as Indian women often do in the privacy of their own lodges.

He maintains his scornful aloofness for a while, trying to make a deal with English and Canadian traders who hang around watching what the Americans are doing. They too have little use for him, and he sees the prospect of a winter with no work. He swallows his pride and through Jusseaume asks the captains to forgive his foolishness and take him back. He promises to do anything they ask.

They sign a contract. He is to receive twenty-five dollars a month in addition to his food for whatever time the trip requires. He is also to be paid for a leather tent which the captains wish to use. Probably it is one Sacagawea and Otter Woman have made.

Charbonneau must really be desperate for work to undertake this difficult journey. Though he has spent many years as a trader among the Indians, his travels have been easy compared to this one. Always he has had a horse to ride and others to carry his trade goods. He has had plenty of food and ample time to lie around his lodge while his wives do the hard work. Most questionable of all is his age. At forty-six he is an old man for this sort of life, twelve years older than Captain Clark, who is otherwise the senior member of the party.

Perhaps the Frenchman longs for association with his kind. Though he has adopted Indian ways, it may be that this winter has roused in him a desire to live once more as a white man. It must be strong to make him willing to undertake the hardships ahead of him.

When Christmas comes, the gate is closed against Indian visitors. They are told that this is one of the big feast days of white people and that they desire to enjoy it alone. Private Joseph Whitehouse, who keeps a detailed journal, describes the celebration:

Tuesday, 25th December, 1804   At half past two another gun was fired to assemble at the dance and So we kept it up

25

*in a jovel manner until eight oC at night, all without
the comp'y of the female Seck, except three Squaws, the
Interpreters wives, and they took no part with us only to
look on.*

One can imagine Sacagawea, Otter Woman, and Madame
Jusseaume sitting in a corner, watching with amazement the
antics of the white men. Music for the dancing is supplied by
Peter Cruzatte and George Gibson, who have brought along
their violins. Others, Sergeant Ordway says in his journal, have
brought "a Tambereen & a Sounden horn," but who performs
on them he fails to report.

On February 11, 1805, Sacagawea's child is born. Indian
women have the reputation of giving quick and easy birth, but
Sacagawea is different. Charbonneau panics, and Jusseaume
is called in to help. The case is unusual, the birth difficult and
prolonged. Jusseaume has never before encountered any such
problem. He fears the girl will die. He goes to Lewis for help,
but this is outside the captain's medical experience also.

Jusseaume remarks that he knows of a remedy, if only he
had the rattles of a rattlesnake handy. Lewis, who has been
busily gathering specimens of plant and animal life to send to
President Jefferson, happens to have some rattles in his collection. He gives Jusseaume two rings which he crumbles
with his fingers and mixes with water. This mixture he takes

to the apparently dying girl and within ten minutes, he reports, the child is born. Lewis comments in his journal that he is skeptical about the value of the remedy, but at least the desired result has followed its use.

The child is a fine boy who is named Jean Baptiste. Sacagawea gives him a name of her own, out of her past. She calls him Pomp, the Shoshone name for leader or head man. Soon everyone is calling him Pomp or, as Americans will, adding the diminutive *ie* sound to make it Pompey. His true name is never given in any of the journals, but Clark mentions it in a letter afterwards.

The winter proves an extremely busy one. In spite of the terrible cold, sometimes as low as forty degrees below zero, the hunters must go out regularly for deer and buffalo. The meat diet is varied by the addition of corn, beans, and squash, which they buy from the Indians.

Every day the fort is thronged with visitors, from whom the captains inquire about the country through which they must pass. The interpreters are kept busy. Charbonneau grumbles to his wives that he has to work too hard. It does not seem to occur to him that when he works, Sacagawea works also, to help him. In spite of this, there must be many hours when the young Indian wives and their children are cooped up together in the tiny hut. They grow lonely for their own kind. All day they hear only the strange English words of the captains and native dialects they often do not understand. Their life is dull and lonely.

Quite likely it is Sacagawea, the youngest, who, after the white men have gone to their quarters for the night, slips out to the big gate and lets in some of their Indian friends. They gather in the interpreters' hut for a visit. Perhaps they chatter too loudly. At any rate, Captain Lewis discovers what they are doing. He rebukes them sternly and posts a sentry so that no Indian may be admitted after the gate has been closed for the night.

On another occasion, Sacagawea steps outside the law to give refuge to an Indian woman who has run to her for protection. Her Mandan husband suspects her, and rightly, of being too friendly with one of the white men and has taken the forthright method of stabbing her to stop the affair. She is streaming blood from her wounds when she rushes into the hut. Her angry husband, knife in hand, comes right in after her and resumes the punishment.

The captains, busy in their own hut, hear the commotion and rush out. Usually they do not interfere with Indian customs, and this time they recognize that according to the red men's rules of conduct, the husband has every right to kill the erring wife. But they will not permit it to happen in their fort, so they manage to calm the man down and send the sinning wife home. The Indian camp is thereafter declared out of bounds for the white men.

Spring comes on slowly, but there is still much work to be done before the party will be ready to resume their journey. The specimens Lewis has so carefully prepared must be as carefully packed to send back to the President. Included are one live prairie dog and four magpies in cages. The prairie dog and one magpie will arrive in Washington safe and well some months later.

The Shoshones have been accustomed to taking their families with them on all journeys except for war. Both Sacagawea and Otter Woman, therefore, expect to go to the Pacific with Charbonneau. They spend the weeks of February and March in making clothing and moccasins for the journey. How much baggage each person is allowed appears nowhere in the journals, but necessarily it is a small amount. The men wrap their bundles in oilcloth, but the Indian women probably prefer a *parfleche*. This is a folding case made of buffalo hide, the Indian version of a suitcase.

Charbonneau, being a white man and a trader, will wear woolen shirts, underwear, and socks, at least until they give out. The women wear the deerskin garments they have been accustomed to all their lives. Sacagawea ties her loose-hanging dress about the waist with a belt of blue beads.

How she has come to own such a treasure, no one now can say. Some writers will suppose that Lewis and/or Clark gave it to her as a present after the birth of her baby. This seems a wild guess, but they may well have paid her with blue beads for making moccasins, mending leather tunics, or some such work. At any rate, she wears the handsome belt with pride, blue beads being those most prized by all Indians.

As a trader's wife she probably owns a thick blanket to wrap around herself and the infant at night. For the daytime, she binds him tightly into a papoose cradle and hangs it over her back. Clark refers to Pompey's carrying case as a "netting," which suggests that it is woven of reeds or strips of bark rather than being a flat board of the kind most often seen.

Having tried out both girls, Lewis chooses Sacagawea as an interpreter to help her husband and says he cannot take Otter Woman. The girls are shocked, but he explains that there is not room in the canoes for an extra person. Otter Woman's little boy would mean an extra mouth to feed, and at some time in the journey she would have to stop to give birth to her expected baby. Sacagawea, on the other hand, will nurse her infant for at least two years, according to Indian custom, so his food will be no problem. She can carry him on her back, so he will require no extra room. Charbonneau pleads that Otter Woman, his favorite, has had one child already, so will cause no delay for the birth of a second, but Lewis still says no. Perhaps he does not want to explain that he has found the younger girl more intelligent than the other.

Later on, when Sacagawea tells the story to a friend, she describes the sorrow of Otter Woman, her weeping day after day and begging to go. Lewis will not relent; indeed, he cannot. A woman's tears cannot be considered, in view of the great task he has undertaken. However, he does agree to pay for Otter Woman's keep while her husband is gone. Still weeping, she is led away to the lodge of the Mandan friends with whom she will live.

By the end of March, the ice leaves the river, and the men carefully calk the two pirogues and the six new canoes they have made. Everything is ready.

The original elements of the great drama have now all come together. The actors wait in the wings, the play is about to begin. But offstage lurk unguessed villains bent on breaking it up—hunger, illness, bitter cold, stifling heat, hostile savages and, above all, the mighty barrier of the Rocky Mountains.

31

PART TWO

THE JOURNEY

OF THESE DIFFICULTIES AHEAD, THE COMPANY
is fortunately unaware on the bright spring afternoon of
April 7, 1805. Final preparations have been completed and the
boats loaded. The keelboat, carrying its reports and specimens
for President Jefferson, pushes off first, headed downstream
for St. Louis. With her go the extra men who were employed
for the winter only and a few Indian chiefs who have been
invited to visit the Great White Father in Washington, D.C.

Headed up the Missouri is the flotilla composed of two
pirogues and six canoes in which thirty-one men, a woman, a
child, and a large black dog are about to attempt the long-
planned dash to the ocean and back. They expect to return to
this place before snowfall.

Charbonneau gives Sacagawea the order to leave. She

swings her baby over her back, picks up the bundle or *parfleche* containing the family's clothing, and obediently walks down the riverbank to the white pirogue to which she and her husband have been assigned. Until this moment her life story is mostly legendary, but as she steps over the gunwale of the pirogue, unnoticed by anyone, she enters the pages of history.

Of her coming importance, neither she nor any of those with her have the least intimation. To them she is merely Charbonneau's "squar," who is likely to be something of a nuisance. Not even Captain Lewis feels too happy about having a woman along, though he is the one who invited her. Only his anticipated need for someone to interpret the language of the Shoshone or Snake Indians and help him get horses for the portage over the expected twenty miles of land between the Missouri and Columbia waterways would have persuaded him to take her. Probably he has given strict orders that there is to be no communication between his men and the young woman. She has a jealous husband, and he wants no trouble to develop. Quite likely he has also told Charbonneau that he and his wife are to keep to themselves while in camp.

What the sixteen-year-old girl thinks as she sits down in the boat is anybody's guess. Her mood is no doubt a mixture of fear and anticipation. Perhaps she will see some of her own people again. Or will all those she loved be dead? Will the ugly old man to whom she was betrothed claim her as his wife?

Probably, in spite of her apparent calm, she is excited with the thought of moving, going somewhere, as she had been in childhood. Probably, at this moment, she is less of Sacagawea, the Bird Woman, and more of Grass Woman, once more started on an adventure. One can only guess; there is no one to whom she can confide her feelings.

To add to her aloneness, not a single person in the party can speak her language. In the months she has lived in the interpreters' hut, she has heard mostly French, the language of her husband and the trader Jusseaume. She can understand it to some extent, but has not learned to speak it herself.

Most of all, she misses Otter Woman, her companion from childhood days, the one who always understood not only her language but her feelings. Now she is to hear no conversation but the few English words spoken by the white captains and the brusque orders of her husband. The men are too busy with their hard work to spend any time in idle talk. For hours on end she hears only the rush of water along the sides of the pirogue, the cries of birds, and the occasional bark of Captain Lewis's dog. She is shut up within herself, uncertain as to how the men feel about her or of what the future may hold for her and her child.

She knows that he is not a welcome guest on this journey. She must, therefore, try in every way to keep him quiet, and, so far as possible, unnoticeable. If she feels, through his wrappings, a restless squirming preliminary to a cry, she loses no time in swinging him around and putting him to her breast. Whenever possible, she gets out of the boat to walk on shore and give him a change of position. At night, she takes off his wrappings, washes and rubs him, then packs him in clean, dry moss to make him more comfortable. She croons him to sleep with the secret love words of her own language that her mother whispered to her.

All this she accomplishes so quietly that the men hardly know she is there. At night, when they prepare to write in their journals, their minds go back over the day to recall difficulties and events they deem of importance. They have no time, paper, or ink for ordinary things. Sacagawea is so little trouble that weeks often go by with no mention of her.

The company is well organized. Each of the sergeants, John Ordway, Nathaniel Pryor, and Patrick Gass, commands a squad of seven or eight men who camp and eat together, separate from the others. Most of the time they camp without shelter. Only when the weather is very bad do they bother to throw a length of oilcloth over a pole for a makeshift tent.

The two captains sleep in the leather tent or tepee they bought from Charbonneau. They carry poles with which it can be set up quickly. Probably Sacagawea helps with this work, since it is one of the customary duties of Indian women. Lewis describes the tent as a large circle of leather which can be folded flat into a quarter-circle and easily packed.

The captains share the tent with the two interpreters, Drewyer and Charbonneau, whose services they may require at any time, the Indian woman and her child, and York. Scammon keeps watch outside. Pomp is evidently a good sleeper, since no mention is made of his crying. Only later, during Sacagawea's one illness, do the captains report that they are kept awake at night.

These same individuals who share the tent also ride in the captains' boat, the white pirogue. It is the best and safest of their flotilla. Sacagawea is given a place in it not because she is a woman or because of the baby but simply because she is the wife of the interpreter. Her place, Clark says, is in the bottom of the boat, near the middle, open to sun, wind, and rain. Here she sits all day. Here little Pomp rides, exposed to all sorts of weather. If it rains, Sacagawea probably swings him around under her blanket. If the sun is too hot, the same blanket makes a shade for him. The only persons who have any shelter are the captains, who have rigged an awning over their seat in the stern.

Only one other man is mentioned as being regularly assigned to the white pirogue. He is Cruzatte, the best waterman of the crew. He is the bowsman and chooses the channel through rapids and mingled currents. Perhaps Joseph Whitehouse is also one of those to help row or pole this boat, since he mentions Sacagawea several times in his journal. When Lewis goes on one of his frequent side trips, he seems to like the company of young George Shannon, Hugh McNeal, and the Fields brothers, Reuben and Joseph. Perhaps he also chooses them to be the crew of his boat. It is merely a guess, but a likely one.

The journals make it clear that Lewis pays very little attention to the Indian woman. He has too many other more important things to take his time and thought. The main responsibility for the success of the expedition is his.

Clark, who carries a little less of the responsibility, is more thoughtful of the girl. He understands how cramped she must become, sitting all day in the bottom of the pirogue with bales and bundles piled around her. He, himself, feels the need to get out and walk along the shore now and then. So he often invites the interpreter and his wife to walk with him. He is more tolerant of the Frenchman than is Lewis. As time goes on, he seems even to like the surly, conceited fellow. Perhaps he feels a grudging admiration for the middle-aged man's ability to endure the hardships that keep much younger men in a state of exhaustion.

Like the others, Charbonneau has to take his turn wading waist-deep in the icy water when it is necessary to pull the pirogue over sandbars or shoals. His feet become cut and bruised from the rocks of the riverbed; the roiling water causes sores and boils on his legs. It is not strange that when night comes he is worn out and cross. In his customary fashion, he takes out his misery on his wife, who is also exhausted and irritable. They quarrel, but Clark does not interfere unless Charbonneau strikes her, as he occasionally does. This the white man cannot permit and so informs the angry Frenchman.

For the most part, however, the girl must look out for herself. Long before this, she has learned to accept what comes, keep silent, and not let her feelings show in her face or actions. She must see, however, that Lewis and Clark live by different standards than anything she has ever known, even living with a white man.

Never before has she been treated with the respect the two captains, especially Clark, show for her. Quite naturally, she becomes devoted and loyal to them. There is, however, no basis for the fanciful assumption some persons will make that Clark falls in love with her, or she with him. He does feel sympathy for her. He thinks of her as a person, a human being, rather than as an animal, the usual estimate of Indian women. Whenever he can, he tries to help her.

The two captains are unlike also in their feelings about the baby. Perhaps this comes from the difference in their backgrounds. Lewis has lived among adults and concerned himself with affairs of state. Clark comes of a big, warm-hearted family in which the sons and daughters, grandsons and grand-daughters, all live in the family home or near it. He has nieces and nephews of whom he is fond and has probably, all his life, played with babies and small children. Little Pomp appeals to his paternal instincts.

We are not told that he strolls over to the Charbonneaus' fire and takes Pomp on his knee, but it is probable. By the end of the journey he will want to adopt him and rear him as his own. Such a feeling does not spring suddenly into a man's mind.

He describes the boy as beautiful and intelligent. Perhaps he shows his French blood more than the Indian. At any rate, throughout the journey it is Clark who shows interest in him and compassion for Sacagawea, though always respecting her as the wife of another man. Furthermore, he compels the same respect from his men.

The white pirogue, because it is the best of the boats, carries the most valuable cargo—the packages of medicines, Captain Lewis's instruments for taking temperatures of air and water and for making astronomical observations, the canisters of lead that hold the irreplaceable gunpowder, and the precious bundle of notebooks in which the captains keep their records.

Years later, when Sacagawea is telling a friend of this

journey, she will say that as she sits in the crowded boat and observes the back-breaking toil with which the men force the craft against the current of the mighty Missouri, she wonders why they do not travel easily on horseback as do her people. She does not speak of this, since she knows no English nor, if she did, would she at this point dare to suggest such a thing to the captains. She does not know nor would she understand Captain Lewis's belief in a waterway across the continent, which he is trying to prove. But if she dared and could speak their language, she thinks she could save the white men much toil and time.

In the preceding months, Captain Lewis has changed his estimate of the distance he will have to travel. During the winter at Fort Mandan, he and Captain Clark have talked with many Indians who know something about the upper river. From these bits of information, Clark has put together a map which will prove surprisingly accurate, showing every stream that enters the Missouri and its approximate location. The two men know, now, that the distance is much greater than they had thought. They are not far from right in believing it to be about two thousand miles.

They still have not the faintest conception of the height and ruggedness of the Rocky Mountains. Lewis thinks they can make an average of twenty or twenty-five miles a day. At even the lower figure, he believes they will be able to complete the return trip in six or seven months. Perhaps he has confided this estimate to President Jefferson. Perhaps this is the reason the President does not send a supply ship around by sea to meet the travelers at the mouth of the Columbia, an error that will very nearly prove fatal to the expedition.

All this is still in the future on that April day of 1805 when the flotilla leaves Fort Mandan. Lewis chooses this time to walk along the shore with his dog, his companion on many of his solitary exploring trips. Always he is observing the nature of the country and its suitability for trading posts, while he gathers specimens of plant life to take home to the President.

He is something of a philosopher, and on this occasion he cannot refrain from congratulating himself on the success of his efforts thus far. This first night, by the light of his campfire, he writes:

Our vessels consisted of six small canoes and two large pirogues. This little fleet, altho' not quite so respectable as those of Columbus or Captain Cook, were still viewed by us with as much pleasure as those deservedly famed adventurers ever beheld theirs; and I dare say with quite as much anxiety for their safety and preservation. . . . However, entertaining as I do the most confident hope of succeeding in a voyage which had formed a darling project of mine for the last ten years, I could not but esteem this moment of my departure as among the most happy of my life.

He might not be so happy on this April evening if he knew it will be seventeen months before he returns to this place.

Everything known about Sacagawea for these seventeen months is to be found in or deduced from the few comments about her in the journals of the two captains plus those of Sergeants Patrick Gass and John Ordway and Private Joseph Whitehouse.

When one considers that the journals are written at night by the light of flickering campfires, after days that last from first dawn to dark, every moment filled with exertion of the most extreme sort, it is amazing that they are kept at all. Only the events of the day that remain in the minds of tired men rate space in their notebooks.

The person who sits quietly, who is not sick, and who does nothing outstandingly good or bad gets no mention. Such a person is Sacagawea, who is with the expedition but not, as yet, of it. Whenever she can, she walks on the shore. It is then that her Indian lore comes in handy. She has knowledge that the white men, for all their superior skill, do not possess.

Quietly she selects a sharp stick and begins poking into a

pile of driftwood. Perhaps the men laugh as they watch her. What is the silly squaw trying to do? She bends over the hole she has made, gathers some small objects into the bag she makes of her deerskin dress, brings her find to York, the captains' cook, and shows him how to boil the objects she has found. Her husband receives his share with no comment other than a grunt of satisfaction as he eats, but surely Clark says, "Good, Janey." A gleam comes into her black eyes, but she allows no smile to curve her lips. It is not good to let a jealous husband see that she likes the praise of other men. Even Lewis is sufficiently impressed to record in his journal that night:

Tuesday, April 9, 1805   When we halted for dinner the squaw busied herself in searching for the wild artichokes which the mice [probably gophers] collect and deposit in large hoards. this operation she performed by penetrating the earth with a sharp stick about some collections of driftwood. her labour soon proved successful, and she procured a good quantity of these roots.

A week or so later comes the first of Clark's walks with the Charbonneau family:

Thursday, April 18, 1805 [Clark]   After brackfast I assended a hill and observed that the river made a great bend to the South. I concluded to walk thro' the point about 2 miles and take Shabono with me . . . his squar followed on with her child, when I struck the next bend of the river could see nothing of the Party, left this man & his wife & child on the river bank and went out to hunt.

When left alone, what do Charbonneau and Sacagawea say to each other? Does he sometimes take the baby in his arms and talk to him? We do not know. It would be good to think he does care about the child and will show it when no one else is around.

Soon the party encounters an unexpected hazard which will haunt them throughout the journey:

Friday 19 April [Ordway]   *the Sand blew off the Sand bars & beaches so that we could hardly See, it was like a thick fogg.*

The men complain of pain in their eyes from this blowing sand. Captain Lewis, who has had a very little medical training, makes a solution of two grains of white vitriol and one grain sugar of lead in one ounce of water. This "eye water" gives some relief and is used constantly by both white men and the Indians, who also suffer from the sandy "fogg."

The weather is miserable; the dog learns a way to hunt antelope.

Saturday 20 April [Ordway]   *High squawls of wind and flights of rain & Snow this day. we took in Some water in the Canoe I was in, the water came up to my Box So that a part of my paper Got wet.*

  Fri. 26th April 1805 [Ordway]   *Saw a flock of Goats [antelope] Swimming the river this morning near to our camp. Capt. Lewises dog Scammon took after them caught one in the River. Drowned & killed it and Swam to Shore with it.*

On this same day they arrive at the mouth of the Yellowstone River. In celebration, Ordway says,

our officers Gave out a Gill of ardent Spirits per man. So we made merry fidled and danced &C.

Both Captain Lewis and Scammon enjoy their walks on shore. One day they are startled by the addition of another fellow-traveler:

Monday, April 29 [Lewis]   *Walking on shore this evening I met with a buffalo calf which attatched itself to me and continued to follow close at my heels until I embarked and left it. It appeared allarmed at my dog which was probably the cause of it's so readily attatching itself to me.*

Scammon seems to enjoy the free life of the prairie almost too much at times and gives his owner much worry.

Thursday, April 25, 1805 [Lewis]　*My dog has been absent during the last night and I was fearfull we had lost him altogether, however, much to my satisfaction he joined us at 8 O'clock this morning.*

The dog becomes more and more daring. On the same day, Lewis reports:

The Antelopes are yet meagre and the females are big with young: the wolves take them most generally in attempting to swim the river; in this manner my dog caught one drowned it and brought it on shore; they are but clumsy swimmers tho' on land when in good order they are extreemly fleet and dureable.

　Sunday, May 5, 1805 [Lewis]　*The party killed two Elk and a Buffaloe today, and my dog caught a goat which he overtook by superior fleetness.*

Then Lewis adds, lest he seem to brag,

the goat it must be understood was with young and extremely poor.

Still, the weather remains cold and miserable.

Friday, May 3 [Ordway]   *clear but very cold for May. Saw the Standing water froze over the Ice froze to our poles . . . and a hard white frost last night the ground covered with Snow.*

Almost a month passes between mentions of Sacagawea. Yet she is a real human being and her child a real, live baby. They are as wet and cold as anyone in the party. The baby is hungry at intervals and must be fed; he must be unwrapped and cleaned at night, taken up and wrapped again in the morning. Yet so quietly and unobtrusively does Sacagawea handle him that the men are not disturbed. They say nothing about him in their journals. Neither do they mention any further efforts on her part to find plant food for them. Soon, however, the time comes when she is useful in a more important way.

It happens on May 14, little more than a month since they left Fort Mandan. The morning has been cold and foggy on the river, the temperature standing at thirty-two degrees. Some of the men go on shore to hunt; even the two captains leave the boat. Late in the afternoon, only a few men and Sacagawea are named as being left in the white pirogue, which is sailing along nicely with a wind from the southwest and the big sail set to catch it. Drewyer, who usually steers, has handed over the helm to Charbonneau, and Peter Cruzatte is in the bow.

Sacagawea has taken advantage of the absence of both Lewis and Clark to move back to the stern in the shade of the awning, her baby still on her back.

Suddenly a strong gust of wind strikes the sail broadside and turns the pirogue over so far it begins to fill with water. Charbonneau panics, lets go the rudder, and begins to pray loudly. Lewis tells the story:

Charbonneau cannot swim and is perhaps the most timid waterman in the world; perhaps it was equally unlucky that Captain Clark and myself were both on shore at that moment, a circumstance which rarely happened; and though we were on the shore opposite to the pirogue, were too far distant to be heard or to do more than remain spectators of her fate.

In this pirogue were embarked our papers, instruments, books, medicines, a great part of our merchandise and in short almost every article indispensably necessary to . . . the enterprise in which we are now launched to the distance of 2200 miles. . . . The steersman, alarmed, instead of putting her before the wind, luffed her up into it. The wind was so violent that it drew the brace of the squaresail out of the hand of the man who was attending it and instantly upset the pirogue and would have turned her completely topsy-turvy, had it not been for the resistance made by the awning against the water. . . . *Captain Clark and myself both fired our guns to attract the attention if possible of the crew and ordered the halyards to be cut and the sail hauled in, but they did not hear us. Such was their consternation at this moment, that they suffered the pirogue to lie on her side for half a minute before they took the sail in. The pirogue then righted but had filled within an inch of the gunwale. Charbonneau still crying to his god for mercy, had not yet recollected the rudder, nor could the repeated orders of the bowsman, Cruzatte, bring him to his recollection until he threatened to shoot him instantly if he did not take hold of the rudder and do his duty.*

Two men seize kettles and begin to bail, while others row slowly to shore. Sacagawea, sitting in the stern, reaches out and catches floating articles as they go by. Says Clark, with characteristic understatement:

This accident had like to have cost us dearly.

Lewis recalls his impulse to jump into the river and try to swim to the pirogue. As he says:

Had I undertaken this project, there was a hundred to one but what I should have paid the forfit of my life for the madness of my project, but this had the perogue been lost, I should have valued but little.

Once the men have reached shore, they drag the boat up on the bank and remove everything, open the bales, and spread the goods to dry. Whitehouse says,

Found that most of the loading was wet, the Medicine Spoiled or damaged very much. Some of the paper and nearly all the books got wet, but not altogether Spoiled.

Two days later, after the contents of the boat have been dried and repacked, the captains find the loss not so bad as they had feared. A few medicines are ruined, and they have lost some garden seeds, also a small quantity of gunpowder. Several cooking utensils which fell overboard sank to the bottom. Otherwise, everything is safe. Lewis gives the Indian girl credit for helping:

The Indian woman to whom I ascribe equal fortitude and resolution with any person on board . . . caught and preserved most of the light articles which were washed overboard.

What these light articles were, he does not mention. Perhaps some bundles of clothing or packages of medicinal herbs—anything that will float. Without her valiant reaching for them, they would have been lost.

Lewis also comments on the fact that without the quick action of Cruzatte, three other men on board, none of whom can swim, would have perished. He does not mention Sacagawea. Perhaps she can swim, but if a strong swimmer like Lewis dared not plunge into the river, her chances would have been small, handicapped as she would be with a baby on her back. The captains do feel grateful to her, however, and a few days later reward her in a special way:

May 20 [Biddle]   A hansome river about 50 yds wide, which we named after Charbonneau's wife, Sahcahjahweah or Birdwoman's river.

Like many other lonely men, Lewis takes great comfort from his dog. Now comes a crisis in the animal's life:

Sunday, May 19, 1805 [Lewis]   One of the party wounded a beaver and my dog as usual swam in to catch it; the beaver bit him through the hind leg and cut the artery; it was with great difficulty that I could stop the blood; I fear it will yet prove fatal to him.

For ten days, readers of the journals are left to wonder about Scammon, whether he is alive or dead. Then comes news:

Wednesday, May 29 [Lewis]   Last night we were all allarmed by a large buffaloe Bull, which swam over from the opposite Shore . . . ran up the bank in full speed directly towards the fires and was within 18 inches of the heads of some of the men who lay sleeping . . . when he came near the tent, my dog saved us by causing him to change his course.

or, as Clark puts it in his note for that day,

our Dog flew out.

So all dog lovers can rest easy; good old Scammon is still able to "fly out" in defense of his master after having the artery of one leg severed only ten days before.

Earlier in this same day, the expedition has happened upon the remains of a large camp of Indians. Fire-blackened spots show that one hundred and twenty-six lodges have been here as recently as two weeks before. Captain Clark also finds the evidences of another large encampment nearby, probably of the same band. Who are they?

Now comes the first official service given by Sacagawea. They take her to the campsite and ask who these Indians were. Through long training, she probably keeps her face expressionless, but her hope soars that her own people are nearby. Eagerly she examines articles found on the campground. As quickly as it rose, hope dies.

Wednesday, May 29 [Lewis]   The Indian woman with us examined the mockersons which we found at these encampments and informed us they were not of her nation, the Snake Indians. She says that her nation make their mockersons differently.

The disappointment for Lewis is also strong. Had these Indians been Shoshones, he might soon have found them and bargained for horses to take them from this point. Clark strikes a happier note by naming the river entering the Missouri near this Indian camp, the Judith, for Miss Julia Hancock of Virginia, who will later become his wife.

A few days later, the party arrives at the mouth of a large river coming from the north. For several days the captains are not sure which of the two branches is the true Missouri. Lewis, with a party of men, explores the northern branch; Clark and another party, the southern. They correctly decide that the southern branch is the main stream. Then Lewis, taking his cue from Clark's recent naming of a river for his sweetheart, gives this fine northern fork of the Missouri the name of Maria's River, for Miss Maria Wood. In a mild apology, he says:

> *It is true that the hue of the waters of this turbulent and troubled stream but illy comport with the pure celestial virtues and amiable qualifications of that lovely fair one: but on the other hand it is a noble river.*

The two names will remain on the map of the United States, one, the Judith, celebrating the happy marriage Clark will make a few years later; the other, Marias River, marking the frustration of Lewis's hopes. Miss Wood will marry someone else, and Lewis will remain a bachelor to the end of his short life.

The expedition continues to move up the main stream of the Missouri. On June 10 they reach the foot of the great falls. Lewis has been scouting ahead and has discovered five main falls within eighteen miles. The pirogues can go no farther.

Monday, June 10th [Whitehouse]   *We halled up the red pirogue on an Island . . . which was covered with Small cotton* [cottonwood] *timber. We halled it among the thickest trees and ran the bow between two & pined her on each side and covered hir over with bushes ... branded several trees with the U.S. mark & Capt. Lewis and Lat'd etc.*

A few days later,

in the morning all hands halled out the white perogue, in a thicket of bushes below the bank and covered hir with bushes.

Captain Lewis takes a party with him to survey the falls and plan how best to move their six canoes around them. All know that from this point on, traveling will be much more difficult. As yet, however, the captains have not given up the hope that most of the journey can be made by water.

Throughout the journals run frequent references to the many illnesses and accidents suffered by the men. They cut and bruise their feet and legs, develop painful boils and what the captains call "tumers"; most frequently, they suffer from digestive troubles. This is not strange, considering the poor food they often have to eat; meat sometimes spoiled, plants and roots that do not agree with them, water polluted by animals or heavy with chemicals.

Sacagawea's childhood experience of a changing diet now

stands her in good stead. Only once in the entire journey, except for a brief bout of seasickness when they come to the ocean, is she sick enough to have the fact noted in any of the journals. This illness begins on June 10, the same day they decide to put the red pirogue in storage. She has violent stomach cramps and high fever and cannot retain any food. In a later day, her illness might be called intestinal influenza.

Lewis has started on with his party to investigate the falls situation, so Clark has to be the doctor. He moves the girl into the back part of the white pirogue, where there is shade under the awning, then applies the only remedy he knows. This is to bleed her, a treatment at this time in vogue for all kinds of illness. At first, it seems to give her some relief, but this is only temporary. For ten days the men despair of her life. They cannot stop, however. While Lewis is gone, they are supposed to move up closer to the falls. Sick or well, the girl must keep going.

What happens to little Pomp during these ten days? Even in her illness, Sacagawea has to nurse him, since he has no other source of food. Who washes and comforts him? Can it be his father? We do not know; he is not mentioned. Perhaps it is Clark, who is much concerned for the mother's comfort and surely for that of the baby. Clark has other medical problems also and even at night cannot get any rest.

June 14, Friday   The Indian woman complaining all night and excessively bad this morning. her case is somewhat dangerous two men with toothake 2 with Tumers & one man with a Tumer and a light fever.

He thinks of quinine bark, boils up some and applies it to Sacagawea externally. The heat helps a bit, but by evening she is worse again and refuses to take any medicine. Her husband has had enough and proposes that they go home. All that holds him is his contract.

Unknown to Clark or Sacagawea, Lewis is suffering from the same form of illness. Traveling light on this reconnoitering trip, he has taken no medicines with him so has to improvise:

Tuesday, June 11   About dinner time I was taken with such violent pain in the intestens that I was unable to partake of the feast of marrow bones. Having brought no medicine with me I resolved to try an experiment . . . the Choke cherry which grew abundantly in the bottom first struck my attention. I directed a parsel of the small twigs to be gathered, striped of their leaves, cut into pieces of about 2 inches in length and boiled in water until a strong black decoction of an astringent bitter taste was produced . . . by 10 in the evening I was intirely releived from pain . . . my fever abated . . . and I had a comfortable and refreshing night's rest.

By the end of the week Lewis has recovered. He comes back to the main camp and discovers how very ill the Indian girl is. He is filled with concern. She is their only hope for talking with the Snake Indians, whom they hope to meet before long, from whom they must get horses if they are to cross the mountains. He is also touched by the girl's misery and the helplessness of the baby. What to do? Apparently there are no chokecherry bushes in this area, so he cannot use the remedy that helped him.

Suddenly he remembers that Indians at Fort Mandan have told him about a spring of sulphur water near the great falls. As a last resort, he determines to try the water of this spring as a cure for Sacagawea. It is on the opposite side of the river, but Clark volunteers to bring supplies of water across. As Lewis tells it:

Capt. Clark now passed over the river and fixed a camp . . . one of the small canoes was left . . . in order to pass and repass the river . . . to procure the water of the Sulpher spring, the virtues of which I now resolved to try on the Indian woman . . . I caused her to drink the mineral water altogether.

In her delirium, she does not want to take the sulphur water, but the captain calls in her husband, who finally persuades her to try it. The treatment soon begins to produce results.

Monday, June 17 [Lewis]   The Indian woman much better today; I have still continued the same course of medicine; she is free from pain clear of fever, her pulse regular and eats as heartily as I am willing to permit her of broiled buffalo well seasoned with pepper and salt and rich soupe of the same meat; I think therefore that there is every rational hope of her recovery.

Tuesday, June 18 [Lewis]   The Indian woman is recovering fast she set up the greater part of the day and walked out for the first time since she arrived here; she eats hartily and is free from fever or pain. I continue the same course of medicine and regimen except that I added one doze of 15 drops of the oil of vitriol today about noon.

The next day Sacagawea is up early, glad to be outdoors again. Clark is also up early and once more asks her for information.

Wednesday, June 19th [Lewis]   This morning early Captain Clark saw . . . where the natives had peeled the bark off the pine trees. this the Indian woman with us informs they do to obtain the sap and soft part of the wood and bark for food.

Another example of the straits in which the Shoshones are sometimes placed to obtain food. Perhaps it is the sight of the pine trees that stimulates Sacagawea's hunger. Though Lewis has given Charbonneau strict orders as to what his wife can eat, and how much, the Frenchman pays no attention or, worse, encourages her to eat more. The result is disastrous:

The Indian woman was much better this morning she walked out and gathered a considerable quantity of the white apples [a succulent root growing in quantities in this area] of which she eat so heartily in their raw state together with a considerable quantity of dried fish without my knowledge that she complained very much and her fever again returned. I rebuked Sharbono severely for suffering her to indulge herself with such food he being privy to it and having been previously told what she must only eat. I now gave her broken dozes of diluted nitre untill it produced perspiration and at ten P.M. 30 drops of laudanum which gave her a tolerable night's rest.

Sacagawea's groans are not all that disturb Lewis this evening.

After dark my dog barked very much and seemed extreemly uneasy which was unusual with him. I ordered the serg't of the guard to reconnoiter with two men, thinking it possible that some Indians might be about to pay us a visit, or perhaps a white bear [grizzly]; he returned soon after and reported that he believed the dog had been baying a buffaloe bull which had attempted to swim the river just above our camp but had been beten down by the stream landed a little below our camp on the same side and run off.

A typical day for Captain Lewis.

With Sacagawea on the road to health, so that Lewis can once more count on her help when he reaches her people, he turns to his other immediate problem—how to transport baggage and canoes around the eighteen miles of falls. The canoes are too heavy to be carried on the shoulders of his men, rugged though they are.

What they need, and therefore must build, are wagons. But how, when there is only a little scrub timber anywhere near? The search parties go out, looking for trees. After a hard scramble,

We were fortunate enough to find one cottonwood tree . . . large enough to make our carriage wheels, about twenty-two inches in diameter; fortunate I say because I do not

believe that we could find another of the same size perfectly sound within twenty miles of us.

They fell the tree and saw its trunk into sections for wheels. For axles, they cut up the mast of the white pirogue. Of the simple parts thus procured, they make two rude wagons or boat carriers and begin the tremendous effort of transporting six canoes and all their supplies, except for a small quantity buried in caches for the return journey. Lewis stakes out the route, and the men set up several camps, shuttling the loads from one to the next.

The banks of the river are cut by deep gullies, so they must constantly be going up or down steep grades. Either way requires such extreme effort that when they pause for a brief rest, the men instantly fall asleep where they stand. To make things worse, the ground is covered with prickly cactus, the spines so tough they penetrate even the thick buffalo-hide soles they have sewed on their moccasins. Their feet are always raw and bleeding.

They must also be on constant guard against the many grizzly bears that abound here. Even the dog Scammon understands the danger of these beasts.

Thursday, June 27 [Lewis]   My dog seems to be in a constant state of alarm with these bear and keeps barking all night.

*Friday, June 28   The white bear have become so trou-
blesome to us that I do not think it prudent to send one man
alone on an errand of any kind, particularly where he has to
pass through the brush . . . they come close around our
camp every night but have never yet ventured to attack us
and our dog gives us timely notice of their visits, he keeps
constantly padroling all night.*

No mention is made of Scammon's attitude toward the baby,
but Newfoundland dogs are generally fond of children. Pomp
is now almost six months old. He no longer lies quietly on his
mother's blanket before the fire, but rolls around and even sits
up a bit. It is not hard to suppose that the big dog comes close
to let the baby pat him and pull his ears, or that part of his
"padroling" is to protect this helpless member of the party.

Since Sacagawea is barely out of danger from her illness,
she is kept at the lower camp to recuperate while the move
around the falls goes on. The weather is hot and humid. In this
almost treeless country there is little shade.

On Saturday, June 29, Captain Clark invites the two Charbonneaus to take a walk with him. Several miles from camp
they see a storm building up and take shelter in a ravine where
shelving rocks make a shallow cave. Here they will be protected from the rain. Sacagawea takes the baby out of his
wrappings to let him cool off.

Suddenly Clark sees a wall of water sweeping down the ravine. He realizes that a cloudburst has struck farther up and that they are in danger of being swept away. He shouts to Charbonneau and grabs Sacagawea, who snatches up her baby, leaving behind his clothing and the woven basket or "netting" as Clark calls it, in which she carries him.

Charbonneau, as usual, freezes in panic, but Clark keeps him moving. He himself pushes the woman ahead of him up the steep bank and comes out on top barely in time to escape the flood. York, who had climbed the hill to hunt, is already safe. They assess their losses. Clark has lost his compass, which he later finds in the mud. The baby's carrying basket and all his clothes are gone. As Lewis reports:

The infant was therefore very cold and the woman also who had just recovered from a severe indisposition was also wet and cold. Capt. C. therefore returned to the camp to obtain dry cloaths.

As soon as the party has established the upper camp, Lewis has part of the men begin a project he has cherished from the time he left Harpers Ferry, Virginia. There he had had made the framework of an iron boat. The pieces have been carried all this distance for assembly when he should reach a suitable place. He plans that once the frame has been put together, he will stretch buffalo hide over it to make a tough, watertight covering. In this canoe he hopes to go to the ocean.

To his great disappointment, no buffalo are to be found here. The men try elk hide but it is too thin and soft. Their awls cut holes too big for the sinews with which they sew the pieces together, so water leaks in. No amount of pitch will keep it out altogether. After three precious weeks have been used in fruitless efforts to make the boat seaworthy, Lewis has to abandon his great project. The men sink the iron frame in the river and go on with the worn wooden canoes.

Scammon continues his favorite method of hunting:

Monday, July 15, 1805 [Lewis]   Drewyer wounded a deer which ran into the river my dog pursued caught it drowned it and brought it to shore at our camp.

Until now, Sacagawea has apparently recognized nothing in the landscape. Not strange, since the Indian trails circled around the great falls, following other streams that led to the Missouri below them. For the first time, the party approaches an area familiar to the girl in childhood. She mentions it to her husband, probably using the Minnetaree language. He communicates the news in French to York or Drewyer who can put it into English for the captains:

Monday, July 22 [Lewis]   The Indian woman recognizes the country and assures us that this is the river on which her relations live, and that the three forks are at no great distance . . . this peice of information has cheered the spirits of the party who now begin to console themselves with the anticipation of shortly seeing the head of the missouri yet unknown to the civilized world.

Mon. July 22 [Gass]   (Approaching Three Forks) At breakfast our squaw informed us she had been at this place before when small.

Wed. July 24   Passed a bank of very red earth which our squaw told us the natives use for paint.

This is the beginning of Sacagawea's so-called guiding, over which writers will argue for many years. All she really does is to identify the river on which her people live. Lewis will naturally follow it in order to meet them. As she predicts, within a week they reach the Three Forks and correctly decide that this is the head of the Missouri proper.

They name the northwest fork, largest of the three, Jefferson, for the President, and decide it is the one to follow. The middle fork becomes the Madison, in honor of the Secretary of State, and the south fork the Gallatin, in honor of the Secretary of the Treasury. Sacagawea remembers that it was here at the forks that she was taken captive.

Sunday, July 28, 1805 [Lewis]   Our present camp is precisely on the spot that the Snake Indians were encamped at the time the Minnetarees of the Knife River first came in sight of them five years since . . . Sahcah-gar-weah our Indian woman was one of the female prisoners taken at that time; tho' I cannot discover that she shews any immotion of sorrow in recollecting this event, or of joy in being again restored to her native country; if she has enough to eat and a few trinkets to wear I believe she would be perfectly content anywhere.

Thus does Lewis reveal the lack of understanding between himself and the Indian girl. In his presence she does not dare let her feelings show. But after long months of silence, this is her moment of glory. She probably tells the story of her capture to different groups of the men.

Tuesday, July 30 [Whitehouse]   At this place our intrepters wife was taken prisoner 4 years ago by a war party of the grossvantors [The Gros Ventres, Minnetarees and Hidatsas are mentioned interchangeably in accounts of this episode] they took hir as she was attempting to make hir escape by crossing a Shole place on the River, but was taken in the middle of it. 2 or 3 Indians killed at the same time on Shore, the rest of the Snakes made their escape.

67

On this same day, Lewis mentions one of the few times he walks on shore with the interpreter and his wife, while Sacagawea reiterates her story:

Tuesday, July 30   Shabono, his woman two invallids and myself walked through the bottom . . . when we again struck it [the river] at the place where the woman informed us that she was taken prisoner.

Probably Lewis now pays more attention to the girl and asks her questions about the country, though she is in no sense guiding the party. They have no other way to go except up the Jefferson River toward the Bitterroot Mountains. A domestic note creeps into the journal of Sergeant Ordway for Wednesday, July 31:

the men not other ways directed are dressing Skins to make themselves mochinsons as they have wore them all out . . . one pair of good mockins will not last more than about 2 days . . . will ware holes in them for the first day and patch them for the next.

Clark is ill again and needs relief from the pitiless heat of the sun.

Thursday, Aug. 1 [Ordway]   *Capt. Clark sick we built a bower for his comfort.*

While Clark recuperates, Captain Lewis takes several men and goes ahead a few days' journey, hoping to find some of the Shoshones. They come to a fork in the Jefferson River where again three branches unite. Lewis is in a philosophical frame of mind. He names one small river the Philosophy. At the forks he christens the north branch the Wisdom and the south, the Philanthropy. The middle one retains the name Jefferson. This one he chooses to follow.

He leaves a note for Clark, telling him which way he has gone, but when the captain arrives at the forks there is no note in sight. Sergeant Gass explains:

Thursday. Aug. 8   We found out the reason why Capt. Clark did not get the note we left at this point, which was that a beaver had cut down and dragged off the pole on which I had fixed it.

Lewis and his party return the same day from a thirty-mile scouting trip up the Jefferson River, having met no Indians. Upon Lewis's return, Sacagawea has more news for him:

Thursday, August 8 [Lewis]   The Indian woman recognized the point of a high plain to our right which she informed us was not very distant from the summer retreat of her nation on a river [Lemhi] beyond the mountains [Bitterroots], which runs to the west. this hill she says her nation calls the beaver's head from a conceived resemblance of it's figure to the head of that animal. she assures us that we shall either find her people on this river or on the river immediately west of it's source [Salmon] . . . it is now all important with us to meet with those people as soon as possible . . . it is my resolution to find them or some others who have horses if it should cause me a trip of one month. for without horses we shall be obliged to leave a great part of our stores, of which it appears to me that we have a stock already sufficiently small for the length of the voyage before us.

The point of land Lewis mentions is Beaverhead Rock, eighteen miles north of the future town of Dillon, Montana.

Obviously, Lewis is beginning to feel worried, though as yet he does not imagine the possibility of giving up the journey to the Pacific. But one thing is sure—he has to get horses, and soon. So he has to find the Shoshones. If ever he thought of Sacagawea as a guide, this would be the time he would take her along to show the way, but he does not do it.

With three men, Shields and McNeal, good hunters, and

Drewyer, who can talk sign language with any tribe, he starts up the Jefferson River, leaving Clark and the rest of the party to follow with the canoes. Clark can hardly walk because of a painful boil or "tumer" on one ankle.

On the first day, Lewis and his companions travel sixteen miles without seeing a single Indian. The second day is a repetition of the first. Lewis observes the river carefully as a prospective transcontinental waterway. This dream he clings to with desperate hope:

Saturday, August 10   I do not beleive that the world can furnish an example of a river runing to the extent which the Missouri and Jefferson's rivers do through such a mountainous country and at the same time so navigable as they are. If the Columbia furnishes us such another example, a communication across the continent by water will be practicable and safe. but this I can scarcely hope from a knowledge of its having in its comparitively short course to the ocean the same number of feet to descend which the Missouri and Mississippi have from this point to the Gulph of Mexico.

The third day, Sunday, August 11, Lewis and his three companions are still searching for Indians. Drewyer walks at some distance to the right and Shields to the left, with Lewis and

McNeal in the middle. After five miles, Lewis sees an Indian on horseback two miles away, easily visible in the open, treeless country. Hopefully he walks toward the Indian, and when he approaches near enough to be seen clearly, he makes the universal sign of friendship. This is to hold up his blanket by two corners, throw it into the air, then to the ground as if spreading it for someone to sit on. The red man pauses, but shows suspicion of Drewyer and Shields, who have not seen him. Lewis signals them to stop, but they do not notice. He calls to the Indian, *"tab-ba-bone"* (white man), and pushes up his sleeves to show he is white though his face and hands are sunburned as dark as the Indian's. He also holds up trinkets and makes signs of giving them to the Indian. However, the two hunters still have not observed his frantic signal and keep on walking toward the Indian, who whirls and rides off.

Much annoyed at Shields and Drewyer, Lewis follows the fleeing red man. He even leaves some small gifts near the breakfast place as a sign of friendship if the man should return. Nothing works, and soon the white men lose the tracks of the horses in the sand and are forced again to take up the weary march. Now they carry a small United States flag on a pole, as a further sign of friendship. Every time they stop to rest, they plant the pole near their camping place. All the rest of that day and the next, their bad luck continues.

They have now reached the head of the Jefferson River, by

this time only a tiny rill emerging from a crack in the rocks. They go through a gap (Lemhi Pass) and find a stream running toward the west. They have crossed the Divide, but their feeling of triumph is tempered by the knowledge that their condition is alarming. Their food is almost gone, and they can find no game.

But Meriwether Lewis is not one to let the mere lack of food keep him from his goal, and his faithful men accept whatever he decides. The following day they resume their march along the Indian road.

Suddenly they see two women, a man, and some dogs a mile away, but they disappear as quickly as the one Indian had a few days before. Lewis tries to capture one of the dogs, intending to tie a handkerchief full of beads and trinkets around its neck, as a message of friendship to the animal's owner. But not even a dog will come near.

The weary, discouraged party rounds a point of land. There, miracle of miracles, beside the road sit three women: an old hag, a young girl, and a child of perhaps twelve years. The young girl runs away, but the other two, thinking their end is near, bow their heads and wait for the expected death blow. Instead, Lewis takes the old woman's hand and lifts her up. Once more he pushes back his sleeve to show his white skin, then gives her and the child some beads, awls, a pewter looking-glass, and some red paint.

At Lewis's request, Drewyer signs to the old woman to bring back the young one. This she does, and Lewis gives her presents also. He spreads vermilion paint on their cheeks, this nation's sign of peace which he probably has learned from Sacagawea. He then asks to be taken to the camp of the chief.

They have not gone far when the chief and two other men, riding in advance of the main body of the Shoshones, appear on the road. When the women show them the presents and tell of the white man's overtures, Lewis relates:

The men then came up and embraced me very affectionately in their way which is by puting their left arm over your wright sholder clasping your back, while they apply their left cheek to yours . . . we wer all carresed and besmeared with their grease and paint till I was heartily tired of the national hug.

All now gather in a circle and pull off their moccasins, their sign of friendship (May I always go barefoot if I am not sincere). After a smoke, they go on to the main camp. The moccasins come off again, and once more the pipe must go around the circle. Lewis gives presents to the head men and asks for food.

Now comes the sad revelation: the Indians themselves are starving. They have nothing but seedy little cakes of dried berries. Their chief, named Cameahwait, owns many horses, but Indians do not eat horses. One kind-hearted native gives Lewis a small piece of boiled antelope meat and a bit of roasted salmon. The latter convinces Lewis they must be on a stream tributary to the Columbia. He has reached his first goal.

Dreams die hard, and Meriwether Lewis is not yet ready to give up his hope of finding a water route across the United States. So far as he knows, this Jefferson River is the most likely possibility. So when on August 8 he started on ahead in search of the Shoshones, he gave orders that the rest of the party should continue to bring the canoes up the Jefferson River. By the time he reached the forks of this stream, he must surely have realized that he had reached the farthest point to which he could travel by water. He therefore wrote Clark two notes and fastened them to a stake (this time one that beavers would not choose) where they would be noticeable. In the notes he asked his friend to wait for him here.

Now, days later and many miles farther up the dwindling Jefferson, he has finally met the Indians. He cannot afford to be separated from them again, but he knows it may be too soon to go back to meet Clark. His own observations have informed him how man-killing will be the task of dragging the heavy canoes to the forks. So he stalls for time by sending his men out to hunt. They return empty-handed, and Lewis cannot stall any longer. He must take the risk of Clark's having been able to keep the rendezvous.

Wednesday, Aug. 14 [Lewis] *I now tell Cameahwait [through Drewyer's sign language] that I wished him to speak to his people and engage them to go with me tomorrow to the forks of Jefferson's River where our baggage was by this time arrived with another Chief and a large party of whitemen who would wait my return at that place. that I wish them to take with them about 30 spare horses to transport our baggage to this place where we would then remain sometime among them and trade with them for horses . . . I promised to reward them.*

He knows the Shoshones have plenty of horses since Drewyer, while out hunting, has observed their herds and has estimated there are about four hundred in this area. Lewis has seen enough of them to know they are good horses, too. He says rather facetiously in his journal that many of them would do honor to the paddocks of Jamestown, Virginia. Each Indian keeps one horse staked near his lodge at night, ready for instant action if needed, since they fight only on horseback.

Well they might, since most of them are undersized, with crooked legs, thick ankles, and thick, flat feet. Yet despite their poverty and poor physical condition, Lewis says they are merry and love dancing, often keeping it up until midnight.

On this same day when Lewis is wondering how to get horses to move all his men and baggage up here to the Indian camp, Clark is having a terrible time beating his way up the Jefferson River. He describes it as "one continued rapid which requires great labour to push and haul the canoes up." In another note he says:

the river obliges the men to undergo great fatigue in the Cold water naked.

Under this strain Charbonneau loses his temper and once more strikes his wife while they are at dinner. She is probably as exhausted as the men. Perhaps the meat is not cooked to suit him, or there may not be enough of it. For whatever cause, he hits her, and Clark leaves his own fire and dinner to break up the quarrel. This is important enough to get into his journal:

I checked our interpreter for striking his woman at the dinner.

Up at the Indian camp, Lewis is having no luck. The Indians are starving and interested in nothing but food. The white men are almost as bad off:

Thursday, August 15 [Lewis]   This morning I arrose very early and as hungary as a wolf. I had eat nothing yesterday except one scant meal of flour and berries except the dryed cakes of berries which did not appear to satisfy my appetite as they appeared to do those of my Indian friends . . . we had only two pounds of flour remaining. this I directed him [McNeal] to divide into two equal parts and to cook the one half this morning in a kind of pudding with the burries as he had done yesterday and reserve the ballance for the evening. on this new fashioned pudding four of us breakfasted, giving a pretty good allowance also to the Chief who declared it the best thing he had taisted for a long time.

Lewis sees that the Indians are reluctant to stay with him any longer. After talking with them in sign language, Drewyer informs him they fear he is in league with their enemies of the plains and plans to lead them into an ambush. In a superb understatement, Lewis writes in his journal,

I readily perceived that our situation was not enterely free from danger.

But he has not come this far only to be denied his goal. Putting on a bold front, he tells Cameahwait, the chief, that he is sorry to find his people resting so little confidence in white men. If this continues, no white man will ever come to trade with them or bring them arms and ammunition:

I [said] I still hoped that there were some among them that were not affraid to die, that were men and would go with me and convince themselves of the truth of what I had asserted.

This speech touches the right spot with Cameahwait, since "to doubt the bravery of a savage is at once to put him on his metal." Cameahwait agrees to go with Lewis to meet the rest of his party, but succeeds in persuading only six or eight of his braves to accompany him. They leave at noon,

old women crying and begging the great spirit to protect their warriors as if they were going to destruction.

With characteristic caprice, the Indians change their minds. In a very short time, Lewis is surprised to find all the men and some of the women following along behind,

now very cheerful and gay, and two hours ago they looked as sirly as so many imps of satturn.

Drewyer, the best of the hunters, goes out again, but once more returns empty-handed. The starving white men cook and eat their last pound of flour, stirred in boiling water.

And away down the Jefferson River, as on many days

before, Clark and his men continue to push and pull the canoes through the shallow water, making slow and painful progress. All those not pulling walk along the shore, including Sacagawea. On this day both she and Clark narrowly escape being bitten by rattlesnakes, which are very numerous near the river.

Lewis, waiting among the Indians, senses the growing danger of his situation. The next morning, Friday the 16th of August, he knows that affairs are approaching a climax. He and his men have absolutely nothing to eat; the Indians also are starving. In desperation, he sends Drewyer out on one more hunt. Unbelievably, he returns with a deer, which he begins to dress.

Word runs like wildfire among the Indians. Mad for food, they rush to the spot where Drewyer is working, snatch up the entrails he has thrown out and stuff them into their mouths. It is a sickening sight to Lewis, who writes:

I really did not untill now think that human nature ever presented itself in a shape so nearly allyed to the brute creation.

He reserves a quarter of the deer for himself and his men, giving the rest to the chief. In their raving hunger, the people tear the meat apart and eat it raw.

Luck has changed. Drewyer brings in another deer, which goes the way of the first; the next morning he shoots a third. The edge of the Indians' hunger is dulled, and they are in a better mood. The whole party, white men and Indians, proceed to the forks of the Jefferson River, where Lewis has promised that his friends will meet him. The wide valley is empty; nobody is there.

At once, Lewis sees suspicion rekindled in the red men's eyes. Any moment they will stop altogether, turn, and leave him. As a final gesture, he gives his gun to the chief and tells him that if he finds he has been deceived he can use it any way he wishes. The men with Lewis likewise hand their guns over to other Indians. Once more a little of the suspicion fades from their faces.

Struggling for time, Lewis thinks of the notes he left for Clark on the way up the river some days before. He walks on a bit, eyes on the bushes near the stream. There are the bits of paper, still tied to the stake. One last possibility occurs to him:

I directed Drewyer to go with an Indian man and bring them to me which he did. the indian seeing him take the notes from the stake on which they had been placed. I now had recource to a strategem in which I thought myself justifyed by the occasion but which I must confess set a little awkward. it had it's desired effect. After reading the notes which were the same I had left I told the Chief . . . that this note was left here today and that he [Clark] informed me he was just below the mountains and was coming on slowly up, and added that I should wait here for him, but if they did not believe me that I should send a man at any rate to the Chief and they might also send one of their young men with him, that myself and two others would remain with them at this place.

Cameahwait, whose name means "One-who-never walks," gives reluctant consent. Lewis writes a note to Clark and orders Drewyer to set out with it early the next morning because there is not a moment to spare. He observes that the Indians are flighty and seem to expect to be attacked in the night.

I knew that if these people left me that they would immediately disperse and secrete themselves in the mountains where it would be impossible to find them or at least in vain to pursue them and that they would spread the allarm to all other bands within our reach and of course we should be disappointed in obtaining horses, which would vastly retard and increase the labour of our voyage and I feared might so discourage the men as to defeat the expedition altogether . . . we finally laid down and the Chief placed himself by the side of my musquetoe bier [net].

I slept but little as might be well expected, my mind dwelling on the state of the expedition which I have ever held in equal estimation with my own existence, and the fait of which appeared at this moment to depend in a great measure upon the caprice of a few savages who are ever as fickle as the wind.

The threads of the drama draw together. The moment for which Sacagawea was born, captured, carried down to the Mandans, and married to the interpreter Charbonneau comes nearer. But the plot has been cunningly conceived, the motives disguised. Nobody, at this moment, even guesses there is a heroine.

All that long night Lewis lies awake wondering whether the hopes and dreams of President Jefferson as well as his own, to say nothing of the expense and labor of the last two and one-half years are to be nullified by the suspicions of the Shoshones. For some reason, he thinks momentarily of the Indian girl, Sacagawea.

I had mentioned to the Chief several times that we had with us a woman of his nation who had been taken prisoner by the Minnetarees, and that by means of her I hoped to explain myself more fully than I could do signs.

So far as we know, the chief was not impressed by this news. Lewis himself may well wonder whether it has been worth the trouble to bring the girl along. Except for recognizing a few landmarks, she has so far been of little help.

Clark, in his camp some distance down the Jefferson River, is also lying awake, beset with problems of a different sort. The river has become so shallow that most of the time it will not float the canoes. Still faithful to Lewis's dream, he has been rotating the crew at the killing job of dragging the heavy boats over the gravelly bottom. The water is icy cold. After an hour's labor the men fall exhausted, but nobody, not even Charbonneau, refuses to take his turn. How much farther can they go under this kind of strain?

In the morning he notices that the men are still stiff, chilled, and fatigued. He decides to let them rest a little longer and enjoy a good breakfast before they start another gruelling day. At seven o'clock, with the thermometer registering forty-eight degrees, they move on.

It is a cold morning for August, and the country is so barren that, when Clark climbs a hill to look around, he can see only three trees in the entire landscape, a fact he confides to his journal.

When Captain Lewis sees the dawn coming, he knows that the fateful morning is here. The crisis has arrived, and no one can longer head it off. He faces it with the same courage he has displayed in all other moments of danger.

Saturday, August 17, 1805 [Lewis]   This morning I arrose very early and dispatched Drewyer and the Indian down the river. Sent Shields to hunt. I made McNeil cook the remainder of our meat which afforded a slight breakfast for ourselves and the Chief. Drewyer had been gone about 2 hours when an Indian who had straggled some little distance down the river returned and reported that the whitemen were coming, that he had seen them just below.

This must seem to Lewis like a death sentence deferred, but what pleases him most is the apparent delight of the Indians:

they all appeared transported with joy and the chief repeated his fraternal hug.

Probably Lewis is too wise to show his pleasure at this point. He has in mind the mercurial temper of the Shoshones and will not permit himself to relax until he is sure of getting horses for his journey.

The big moment of the drama approaches. The stage is the flat, upland plain with only three trees for scenery: the backdrop, the vast blue sky of Montana. The midmorning August sun burns down upon the luckless travelers who a few hours ago shivered in the freezing cold of the mountain night.

At one side stands Meriwether Lewis, unarmed, surrounded by fifty or sixty gaunt, starving, suspicious red men who hold his gun and the weapons of his two remaining companions.

At the other side, William Clark walks slowly, limping from the painful boil on one ankle. Behind him come two dozen almost naked men, divided into small groups, each dragging a heavy canoe by means of a line over their shoulders. What do they think as they approach the much larger party of savages and see their unarmed leader in their midst? Is he their captive? Should they seize weapons and try to rescue him? Even Clark must wonder what his next move should be.

Of the two captains, only Lewis has a strong sense of history. While he stands helpless, waiting for the slow-motion march to come close, it surely must be in his mind that one false gesture on the part of his friends, one hand reaching for a gun, one shot fired, will mean immediate death for himself, Clark, and all their men. That no one will discover for years, or perhaps never, how they have struggled to reach this place.

Even he does not grasp the full significance of the crisis, one of the great turning points of American history. If he and Clark should die here, it will be years before the Congress of the

United States will commit another venture to explore the Rocky Mountains. Thomas Jefferson will not have time to work it up, since he has already begun his second and last term of office as President. He will be succeeded by James Madison, whose interest turns toward Europe and the coming struggle with Great Britain, rather than toward the unknown wilderness west of the Mississippi.

To the north, in Canada, Alexander MacKenzie has already reached the Pacific Ocean by land; Simon Fraser is readying a party for the exploration of the Fraser River; David Thompson hovers about the passes of the Rockies, waiting only for a favorable moment to cross to the Columbia. Less than four years later, he will stand at the confluence of that great stream and its principal tributary, the Snake. There he will affix to a pole a thrifty half-sheet of paper whereon he has written his claim to the whole country in the name of Great Britain.

The principal counter-claim that will stand up in negotiations for possession of this great area, one-third of the continental United States, will be that of Lewis and Clark, who will have reached the Columbia before Thompson. At this moment in the high mountain country, however, that outcome is uncertain.

Lewis, still trying in the face of defeat, orders Drewyer and his Indian guard to advance and greet Captain Clark. To strengthen his companion's belief in his sincerity, Drewyer has changed clothing with him. His black hair and sun-darkened skin make him look so much like an Indian himself that he probably wonders whether his friends will recognize him.

At last the great moment has come. On both sides the actors, trembling with suspense, wait for their cues.

Then from Clark's side of the vast open stage, two persons begin to move toward the center. The girl Sacagawea, baby on back, walks beside her probably protesting husband, ahead of the rest of the party. Did she become impatient with the slow-moving crew pulling the boats and dart out ahead? Did Clark, remembering the rattlesnakes, order Charbonneau to drop the towline and go with her? Does he scold her in scathing French as he limps after her?

She pays no attention. Her feet cannot keep up with her thoughts. Her eyes search the waiting Indians, hoping for some sign. Are these really her people? Will any of them know her? Is she to learn that all of her family are dead? That the other children who were captured with her never reached their home again?

Farthest from her mind and from that of every man watching her is the thought that she is the heroine, moving upstage in a world drama.

Years later, when the journals are being prepared for their first publication, Clark himself will dictate to his editor the story of this hour, in his own vivid language:

Saturday, August 17, 1805 [Clark], (Biddle)   They had not gone more than a mile before Captain Clark saw Sacagawea, who was with her husband one hundred yards ahead, begin to dance and show every mark of the most extragant joy [she who Lewis thinks shows no emotion and cares for nothing but enough to eat and a few trinkets], turning round him and pointing to several Indians, whom he now saw advancing on horseback, sucking her fingers at the same time to indicate that they were of her native tribe. As they advanced captain Clark discovered among them Drewyer dressed like an Indian. While the boats were performing the circuit [around a bend] he went towards the forks with the Indians, who as they went along, sang aloud with the greatest appearance of delight.

We soon drew near to the camp, and just as we approached it a woman made her way through the crowd towards Sacagawea, and recognizing each other, they embraced with the most tender affection. The meeting of these two young women had in it something peculiarly touching, not only in the ardent manner in which their feelings were expressed, but from the real interest of their situation. They had been companions in childhood, in the war with the Minnetarees they had both been taken prisoners in the same battle, they had shared and softened the rigours of their captivity, till one of them had escaped from

*the Minnetarees, with scarce a hope of ever seeing her
friend relieved from the hands of her enemies.*

Leaping-Fish Woman! After all these years! The two cling
together while the rest of the women gather around them, the
white men forgotten in the outpouring of love and joy. Their
Grass Woman, Bo-i-naiv, has come back to them. Immediately,
the two captains feel the change in the attitude of the Indians.
Fear and suspicion give way to surprise, joy and welcome. But
there is more to come. Wonderful as this is, Sacagawea's
heroic role has still the punch line to deliver:

*While Sacagawea was renewing among the women the
friendships of former days, Captain Clark went on and was
received by Captain Lewis and the chief . . . the moccasins
of the whole party were then taken off and after much cere-
mony the smoking began. After this the conference was to
be opened, and glad of an opportunity of being able to converse more intelligibly, Sacagawea was sent for; she came
into the tent, sat down, and was beginning to interpret,
when in the person of Cameahwait she recognized her
brother. she instantly jumped up, and ran and embraced
him, throwing over him her blanket and weeping pro-
fusely; the chief was himself moved, though not in the
same degree. After some conversation between them she*

resumed her seat, and attempted to interpret for us, but her new situation seemed to overpower her, and she was frequently interrupted by her tears. After the council was finished, the unfortunate woman learnt that all her family were dead except two brothers, one of whom was absent, and a son of her eldest sister, a small boy, who was immediately adopted by her.

So the great moment passes into history, but as yet not one of the actors is aware that the drama has reached its climax or even that this is a drama, with world significance. Only later, when historians have had time to study it, will its values be understood. It will then be possible to estimate the importance of the episode, not only to the Lewis and Clark expedition, but to the whole further history of the United States.

At the moment when all the carefully laid plans of President Jefferson and all the tremendous efforts of his able captains hang in the balance, it is the Indian girl who tips the scale. And by no other means than simple identity. By the incredible coincidence that she is the sister of the chief, a coincidence no fiction writer would have dared use, she establishes confidence in both the white men and the Indians.

Without her presence, the Shoshones might yet refuse to sell horses to the captains; the expedition might still fail, even though Clark has appeared as Lewis promised. It is for this moment, and one other still to come, that Sacagawea rates historical importance wherever the names of Lewis and Clark are mentioned. But, like the others, at the moment when it happens, she is unaware of any importance at all.

What matters to her is that she has been returned to her own people and has found some who know her. What a joy to be among those who speak the same language! With pride she shows her friends her beautiful baby and admires theirs. She fondles her sister's little son and sets him beside Pomp on her blanket. At this time, she surely intends to keep him with her. Perhaps she hopes to remain here among her people. Charbonneau is very tired and longs for rest. Here among the Shoshones he can be a big man.

While the women gather in one part of the camp, the men, off in another part, are likewise very gay. The chief promises to go to his permanent camp on the western slope of the mountains and persuade his people to send horses to bring the white men to them.

Clark breaks out the stores from the canoes and serves a big meal of hominy, the first the Indians have ever tasted. They eat with great enjoyment. Both parties then vie with each other in providing entertainment. The Indians put on their tribal dances. The white men also dance, to the music of the violins, "tambereen and sounden horn" they have employed so many times on the journey for their own pleasure. York, a natural comedian, delights the red men with acrobatic stunts, and Scammon shows off all his tricks, the Indians seeming much astonished at a dog so clever.

Suddenly the joyous program is interrupted by the arrival of an ugly old man who has evidently heard of the appearance of the Indian girl. He loudly declares that she belongs to him. He reminds the others that he bought her from her father many years ago.

This is what Sacagawea has feared might happen. Her past returns to haunt her. But she will not yield to her betrothed husband without a fight. She boldly opens her blanket to disclose little Pompey, sleeping in her arms. This is her child, she tells the old man. His father is this white man, Charbonneau.

The husband, who has three wives already, turns away in scorn. Since she has a child by another man, he does not want her. Once more the celebration goes on, in an outpouring of food and good spirits not unlike a modern convention.

The captains withdraw to one side and make plans. The Indians have told them it will be impossible to reach the ocean by way of the Lemhi and Salmon rivers, on whose banks the tribe makes its summer home. Lewis is not willing to accept their verdict without personal investigation by himself or Clark. The latter agrees to go take a look, with Charbonneau and Sacagawea to interpret for him.

They will send men with horses to bring the baggage over

the mountains. By the time Lewis gets there, Clark will have had time to explore the rivers which they know are tributary to the Columbia. In far different spirits than on the preceding night, the white men spread their blankets.

Before Lewis goes to sleep he sits by his candle and philosophizes:

Sunday, August 18, 1805 [*Lewis*]   *This day I completed my thirty-first year, and conceived that I had in all human probability now existed about half the period which I am to remain in this Sublunary world. I reflected that I had as yet done but little, very little, indeed, to further the happiness of the human race or to advance the information of the succeeding generation.* [*How little he realizes the importance of what he is doing on this journey.*] *I viewed with regret the many hours I have spent in indolence, and now soarly feel the want of that information which those hours would have given me had they been judiciously expended. but since they are past and cannot be recalled, I dash from me the gloomy thought, and resolved in future, to redouble my exertions and at least indeavour to promote these two primary objects of human existence, by giving them the aid of that portion of talents which nature and fortune have bestoed on me; or in future, to live for* mankind, *as I have hitherto lived* for myself.

Once across the pass, Clark and his party come to the main camp of the Shoshones. He engages a skilled guide, an old man he calls Toby, and his two sons to take him down the Lemhi and Salmon to study their possibilities.

Part of the Indians, headed by Cameahwait, his sister and her husband, return to Lewis's camp. Word of the fine meals prepared by the white man has made all the Indians eager to taste the good food.

Thursday, August 22 [*Lewis*]   *Charbono, the Indian Woman, Cameahwait and about 50 men with a number of women and children arrived. they encamped near us . . . having no fresh meat and these poor devils half starved I had previously prepared a good meal for them all of boiled corn and beans which I gave them as soon as the council was over and I had distributed the presents. this was thankfully received by them. The cheif wished that his nation could live in a country where they could provide such food . . . I gave him a few dryed squashes which we had brought from the Mandans. he had them boiled and declared them to be the best thing he had ever tasted except sugar, a small lump of which it seems his sister Sah-cah-gar Wea had given him.* [*From her store in the* parfleche *suitcase?*] *. . . I purchased five good horses of him very rea-*

sonably, or at least for about the value of six dollars apeice in merchandise.

Now that he has begun to succeed in getting horses, Lewis evidently thinks that Sacagawea deserves a reward for her help. He gives Charbonneau some merchandise with which to buy a horse for her. What effect this has on her Indian women friends one can only guess. Certainly they must be startled, since in their tribe it is the man of the family who rides if there is only one horse. If he owns a second animal, his wife and children may share rides, unless the horse is too heavily loaded with the family possessions. Possibly the women are jealous of Sacagawea when they see her mounted while they have not only to walk but help carry the white men's baggage as well. Perhaps this is the beginning of her second separation from her people.

Lewis camps at some distance from the Indians so they will not see what he is about to do. At night he has his men dig caches in which to store some of the supplies they will need on the return trip. The cache is a hole shaped like a short-necked bottle with an opening perhaps two feet across in the top. They cut out sod very carefully to make this opening, then scoop dirt from below, disposing of it in the river. When they have a large enough space, they line the hole with dry branches and hides to protect the goods buried there. After they have filled the hole, they replace the sod with great care so the ground looks as before. They make meticulous notes about its location, so they can find it again when they come back.

They also sink their canoes in the river to preserve them from drying out, being ruined by the fires the Indians often set in the forest, or chopped up for firewood.

Though Lewis recognizes that further canoe travel on this side of the mountains is impossible, he clings to the hope that Clark will find the Lemhi and Salmon rivers navigable. It will be a short trip over the pass by using horses to carry their baggage. Then they can make new canoes and still get down to the ocean. By this time, however, he must be aware that he will be unable to return to Fort Mandan before winter as he had planned.

Clark sends word that his Indian guide, while agreeing to take him down the Salmon some distance, still insists that it is too wild for any canoe. What the white men should do, he says, is to journey farther north to another river used by the Nez Percé tribe to go back and forth from the Columbia to the buffalo plains.

Clark assures Lewis he still intends to make the survey, but he is convinced that the Indian is right. He thinks their best chance is to buy enough horses to carry themselves and their baggage to the northern river of which the guide has told him.

For Lewis to accept this plan means abandonment of the dream both he and President Jefferson have held for many years. It is a dream all explorers up to this time have cherished since the earliest discoveries in North America—the dream of a waterway across the continent. However, Lewis knows reality when he sees it. Since he must change and go by land, he begins at once to make the necessary arrangements. The first goal is the camp across the mountains from which they will make their northward push.

It is unfortunate for future historians that Sacagawea does not know how to write, so she cannot leave any record of her feelings during this time. To try to re-create them, one must mentally step into her skin and feel with her the circumstances that now surround her.

After five years of captivity, she is back again among her own people. For these few days, she sheds whatever of white men's ideas have rubbed off on her and becomes all Indian again. She thrills to the story of Leaping-Fish Woman and the other children who escaped from the Minnetarees and successfully made their way home again. Her friends bring her up to date on what has happened within the tribe; she tells them of her life among the Mandans. Together, they weep over poor Otter Woman, left behind to grieve.

Though she has a horse to ride, which sets her above the others, they still trust her as one of them and do not attempt to conceal from her the plans they are making. Perhaps her brother himself tells her what he has decided to do.

It is on Saturday night, August 24, 1805, when she learns that he is about to send a messenger to the rest of the Shoshones on the other side of the mountains, telling them to come at once and join him in a dash to the Missouri for buffalo. What the white men will do is no concern of his.

His decision is not surprising. His people are starving, and even the guns of the white men cannot get deer when there are none. Better to go at once, while the people have strength for the journey. To help the white men might mean death by starvation for many of his people.

This must be the night when Sacagawea in her turn lies sleepless trying to decide what to do. If she passes on to the white chiefs word of her brother's plan, her people will hate her. The love so recently renewed will turn to anger. They will think of her as a traitor. Her own brother will claim her no more. He will not let her have her sister's child to rear.

Every drop of her Indian blood cries out, "You are not Sacagawea, you are Bo-i-naiv, Grass Woman. Stay with your own people where you belong. They did not ask the white men to come here; what happens to them is nothing to you, as you are nothing to them but a convenience, to serve their purposes."

Try as she will, however, the girl cannot forget that she has been Sacagawea, the Bird Woman; she has been out in the world far beyond the places her people know. She has seen the plains Indians with their guns. She has learned how comfortably they live in their warm lodges, with plenty of food to last through even the longest winters.

If her brother deserts these white men, they will die or return to their own country. No one will bring guns to her people so they can compete on even terms with the plains Indians. Always their life will be as she sees it, a struggle merely to keep breath in the starving bodies of men, women, and children. There is no one to whom she can turn for advice; she must make her decision alone.

By morning she has chosen her way. Though she knows she will be an outcast among her own people, she must try to save their future. She still does not know enough English to talk to Captain Lewis herself. Even if she did, she would be too much afraid of him and of what he might do to her brother. So she whispers the news to her husband and asks him to pass it on to Lewis.

Charbonneau grunts and dismisses the matter from his mind. What does a foolish woman know of the plans of her chieftain brother? Hours go by while he keeps silent. Perhaps it is only the nagging of Sacagawea that finally makes him speak:

Sunday, August 25 [Lewis] Sometime after we had halted for dinner Charbono mentioned to me with apparent unconcern that he expected to meet all the Indians from the camp on the Columbia [Lemhi] tomorrow on their way to the Missouri. allarmed at this information I asked why he expected to meet them. he then informed me that the 1st Cheif [Cameahwait] had dispatched some of his young men this morning to this camp requesting the Indians to meet them tomorrow and that himself and those with him would go on with them down the Missouri and consequently leave me and my baggage on the mountain or thereabouts. I was out of patience with the folly of Charbono who had not sufficient sagacity to see the consequences which would inevitably flow from such a movement of the indians, and although' he had been in possession of this information since early in the morning when it had been communicated to him by his Indian woman yet he never mentioned it untill the after noon. I could not forbear speaking to him with some degree of asperity on this occasion. I saw that there was no time to be lost in having these orders countermanded or that we should not in all probability obtain any more horses or even get my baggage to the waters of the Columbia.

Here again Lewis does not mention in his journal, perhaps because he does not even recognize it, how valuable has been the help of Sacagawea in passing this information to him. He has no time or thought for anything except how to persuade Cameahwait to change his mind.

He calls the three principal chiefs together, with Sacagawea and Charbonneau for interpreters. After the pipe has gone around he asks them if they are men of their word and whether he can depend on the promises they have made. They say yes, but Sacagawea probably does not dare raise her eyes to look at her brother. Well he must know how Lewis learned of his plans.

The other chiefs, knowing nothing of the girl's part in the affair, admit to Lewis that they promised to take his baggage to their camp across the mountains or to some other place where Captain Clark might decide to build canoes.

It is well for Sacagawea that she has had long practice in keeping out of her facial expression the feelings in her heart. Her eyes are blank as she interprets what Captain Lewis says:

I then asked them why they had requested their people on the other side of the mountain to meet them tomorrow on the mountain where there would be no possibility of our remaining together for the purpose of trading for their horses as they had also promised. that if they had not promised to have given me their assistance in transporting my baggage to the waters on the other side of the mountain that I should not have attempted to pass the mountains but would have returned down the river and that in that case they could never have seen any more white men in their country. that if they wished the white men to be their friends and to assist them against their enemies by furnishing them with arms . . . that they must never promise us anything which they did not mean to perform . . . and finally concluded by telling them if they intended to keep the promises they had made me to dispatch one of their young men immediately with orders to their people to remain where they were untill our arrival.

No doubt Sacagawea longs to tell her brother why she revealed his plans, but she knows he would not understand. Perhaps he will never understand. Perhaps the white men will not keep their own promises.

Probably her brother does not look at her as he admits to Lewis that it was he who made the decision to leave for the hunting grounds because his people are so hungry. But he is a man of his word; he will keep his promise.

How does he feel as he utters these words to his sister for her to interpret? How does she feel as she puts them into her halting French for Charbonneau to pass on in the broken English he has learned during these months with the white men?

Is she aware that this is the dividing point in her own life? That she has permanently cast her lot with white people? When she leaves the council, does she see the faces of her friends turn away from her? Does one of them pick up her little nephew and carry him to her brother's tent?

The tragedy of Sacagawea at this moment is her aloneness. There is no one to share her sorrow; she has no way of putting it into words for future historians to read. Worst of all, her sacrifice is not even recognized by those who will benefit from it. Perhaps Lewis would be pleased at this moment if she should choose to stay with her own people. For the rest of the journey he could well do without her. He does not understand that she has to go, that she is no longer welcome among them. But so little does he think about her that for six weeks he does not once mention her in his journal.

The party moves on. Many of the Shoshones are still reluctant and angry because of their fierce hunger. What dark glances do they cast in the direction of the girl who has betrayed them, who rides a horse while other Indian women walk? What agonies of separation does Sacagawea endure? We do not know. But from this time on, whenever she does come into the written record, she seems different. No longer is she the timid mouse wanting only to make no trouble. She knows that she has earned her place in the party, and she intends to be recognized as a member of it.

They cross the Bitterroots to the main Shoshone camp where they again meet Clark. He has journeyed seventy miles down the Lemhi and Salmon rivers and has satisfied himself that this route is impossible. The captains bargain with the Indians, their hope being to obtain at least one horse per man, with a few more to carry their packs. They succeed in buying only twenty-nine animals.

Loading their baggage, they start north, guided by Toby. Happily they do not know that the next six weeks will be the most difficult of the entire journey.

Sept. 2, Monday [Clark]   Proceded on thro' thickets in which we were obliged to Cut a road over rockey hill Sides where our horses were in perpeteal danger of Slipping to their certain destruction & up & Down Steep hill Sides, one horse Crippled and 2 gave out.

September 3d, Tuesday . . . in the after part of the day the high mountains closed the Creek in each Side and obliged us to take on the Steep Sides of those mountains, So Steep that the horses Could Scurcely keep from Slipping down . . . but little to eate I killed 5 Pheasants & the

hunters 4 with a little Corn afforded us a kind of supper . . .
This day we passed over emence hils and Some of the worst
roads that ever horses passed.

This is bad enough for vigorous men, but what must it be for
the lonely girl and her baby? Pomp is now seven months old
and a heavy burden whether he rides on her back or is moved
in under her blanket to save him from freezing.

They meet a party of Tushepaw or Flathead Indians who
are friendly but as hungry as the rest.

We spoke to them with much dificulty as what we said had
to pass through Several languages before it got into theirs.

No mention of Sacagawea, though she is probably one of
those through whom the conversation passes, since her language is the nearest to that of the strangers.

On September 9, two weeks after they left the Shoshone
camp, they come to the Hellgate River and a pass through the
mountains which the Indians say leads to the Missouri River.
From this point, they tell Lewis, it is only a five-day journey to
the Missouri, certainly a far cry from the fifty-eight days they
have spent by following the river to its source. If one were to
suppose that Lewis ever thought of Sacagawea as a guide, this

news would be enough to discredit her. There is no evidence that he does now or ever has thought of her in this way. He is interested in the shorter route and determines that when they return, he will try this new way over to the Missouri.

They camp on a creek they name Travellers Rest because they stop for a day or two to rest their horses. Having fulfilled their promise, the main body of Indians leaves for the buffalo hunting grounds. Only old Toby and his sons remain to guide the white men over Lolo Pass, which separates the watersheds of the Clark Fork and Snake Rivers.

At length they come to a creek they name Glade for the beautiful valley through which it runs. Now they know they are on waters of the Columbia system, but there is still much misery ahead of them before they reach the great river itself.

Monday, Sept. 16, 1805 [Clark]   The Knobs, Steep hill Sides & falling timber continue to day, and a thickly tim-bered Countrey of 8 different kinds of pine, which are so covered with Snow, that in passing thro' them we are con-tinually covered with Snow, I have been wet and as cold in every part as I ever was in my life, indeed I was at one time fearfull my feet would freeze in the thin Mockersons which I wore . . . I took one man and proceeded on as fast as I could about 6 miles to a Small branch passing to the right, halted and built fires for the party against their arrival which was at Dusk, verry cold and much fatigued . . . Men all wet cold and hungary.

And among them a baby who must be as wet and cold as the others, but neither he nor his mother make enough fuss to be noted in the journals. The first meal is made on the dried soup they have carried for emergencies, but it is so tasteless and of so little food value they all despise it. Hunger drives them to eat some of their horses, and they begin with the colt, "a coalt being the most useless part of our Stock." The road continues almost impassable.

Thursday, Sept. 19 [Lewis]   Fraziers horse fell from this road in the evening, and roled with his load near a hundred yards into the Creek. we all expected that the horse was killed but to our astonishment when the load was taken off him he arose to his feet & appeared to be but little injured, in 20 minutes he proceeded with his load. this was the most wonderfull escape I ever witnessed, the hill down which he roled was almost perpendicular and broken by large irregular and broken rocks.

They meet the first Nez Percé or Chopunnish Indians, whose chief is named Twisted Hair. These people speak a language very different from the Tushepaws (Flatheads) or

Shoshones. "They are large, Portley men, Small women and handsom featured." They are also intelligent and friendly. They generously share their food, which consists of dried salmon and bread made of the quamash or camas root.

Mad with hunger, the men eat too much, and almost all become very sick. Some are so weak that "they are compelled to lie on the Side of the road for Some time others obliged to be put on the horses." No mention of Sacagawea's being ill. Her childhood training in changing from one diet to another may help her, or it may be that she is accustomed to camas.

The visit of the white men is not entirely a surprise to the Nez Percés. Early in the spring of this year, 1805, three men of their own tribe went east across the mountains and as far down the Missouri as the Hidatsa settlements in North Dakota on a trading trip. There they heard about the white men who already had started up the river with their great supply of trade goods.

No doubt they also heard of the woman who accompanied them, so the appearance of Sacagawea with her child is a means of identification.

Supposedly these or some other Nez Percés, on similar trading trips, have acquired several guns. They are eager to trade for ammunition, so welcome the arrival of the white men.

Another influence toward friendliness with the whites is

the word of an old Nez Percé woman who had once been captured and carried off to Canada. There white men were good to her and gave her medicine for her eye troubles. Having made her way back to her own people, she now tells them to be kind to these white men because white people were kind to her. The captains see her and hear something of her story, but do not know it is she who is partly responsible for their warm reception.

Now that they are down out of the mountains, instead of cold they must endure extreme heat. Moving down the valley of the Kooskooske or Clearwater River, they set up camp opposite the forks at a place which will later be called Canoe Camp.

Captain Lewis himself and most of the men are still sick and weak, but work must go on in spite of it. They bring out the iron axe heads they have carried from St. Louis and fit them with handles. The axes are small and inadequate for cutting the large pine trees, but the men have nothing else to use.

Twisted Hair and his tribesmen show the white men how to burn out the centers of the logs, which speeds up the process of boatbuilding. By October 6 they have finished one small and four large canoes. They catch and brand their horses, then turn them over to Twisted Hair, who promises to care for them during the winter. Once more working in secret, the white men bury two lead canisters of powder, "2 foot 4 In. North of a dead toped pine opposit our camp" for use on the return trip.

The dried fish and camas diet continues to disagree with them, but they have nothing else to eat. On Monday, October 7, they resume the trip down the Clearwater. After two days, Toby the guide and his sons suddenly disappear. Lewis regrets that he has not paid for their services, but is consoled by the probability that if he had, other Indians would soon have stolen whatever merchandise he gave them.

For the first time, the men began to buy dogs for food. (Does Sacagawea eat dog meat? We do not know, but most Indians spurn it.) Lewis develops a liking for it, but Clark will not touch it.

On the tenth of the month they reach the junction of the Clearwater and the Snake. Clark, with his remarkable instinct for geography, recognizes this river as the one to which the Salmon was tributary. They name it Lewis's River.

At last, on October 12, comes the first mention of Sacagawea in six weeks. Clark writes:

The wife of Shabono our interpreter we find reconciles all the Indians, as to our friendly intentions. a woman with a party of men is a token of peace.

So although her most important work is finished, she is yet useful merely by being seen with the white men.

On Wednesday, October 16, they reach the Columbia River and camp on the point which later will become Sacagawea Park. After coming so far to find this great stream, it is surprising that the captains write almost nothing about what must have been an exciting moment. Perhaps it is because the main interest now is centered on food. Fish being out of season, they buy forty dogs and on the 18th, start on down the Columbia. Clark resumes an old habit.

Saturday, October 19 [Clark]   I deturmined to walk down on the Lar'd side with the 2 chiefs [of the Walla Walla Indians] the interpreter & his woman, and directed the small canoe to procede down on the Lar'd Side to the foot of the rapid which was about 2 miles in length. [Umatilla Rapids]

Clark climbs a cliff from which he can see a long way down the river. There he observes the first of the great mountains, Mt. Adams, which he mistakes for Mt. St. Helens.

As they continue down the river, the Indians they meet seem much frightened at the approach of white men, but

as Soon as they Saw the Squar wife of the interpreter they pointed to her and informed those who continued yet [hiding in their lodges] they immediately all came out and appeared to assume new life, the sight of This Indian woman, wife to one of our interpreters, confirmed those people of our friendly intentions, as no woman ever accompanies a war party of Indians in this quarter . . . two of our party, Peter Crusat [Cruzatte] and Gibson played on the violin which delighted them greatly.

On October 23 they portage around the falls at The Dalles. Soon they begin to meet Indians wearing European-style clothing and carrying kettles of brass and copper which could only have come from white men. One of the captains remarks that Charbonneau seems to be very tired. Not strange, considering what this middle-aged man has endured. This is no excuse, however, and Clark has "Some words with Shabono our interpreter about his duty."

Sunday, November 3 [Clark]   A canoe arrived from the village below the last rapid with a man his wife and 3 children and a woman whome had been taken prisoner from the Snake Indians on Clarks River. I sent the Interpreters wife who is a So so-ne or Snake Indian of the Missouri to Speake to this squar, they could not understand each other Sufficiently to converse.

The poor prisoner, separated perhaps for years from her home, looks hopefully to the young Shoshone girl, longing to get news of her people. But even among the Snakes the dialects are different in different areas. The two women try, but cannot make each other understand. The prisoner must continue doomed to ignorance of her home and relatives while Sacagawea, having experienced the joy of return from captivity, cannot help her.

Thursday, November 7 [Clark]   Great joy in camp we are in view of the Ocian this great Pacific Octean which we have been so long anxious to See, and the roreing or noise made by the waves braking on the rockey Shores (as I suppose) may be heard distinctly.

Clark is a little ahead of the facts, since the party is still some miles from the ocean proper. However, they have come into the wide bay at the mouth of the Columbia, they see the rise and fall of the tide and hear the breakers thunder on the beaches. They have reached their goal. Now comes the trying problem of spending a winter here, since it is well into November and they know they cannot re-cross the mountains until spring.

The party must find a place to camp, but this proves very difficult on the north side of the Columbia where they have landed.

Nov. 8 Friday [*Clark*]   *The swells were so high and the canoes roled in such a manner as to cause several to be verry sick . . . the Squar was of the number.*

This is only the second time, but it is the last time for any mention of illness on the part of Sacagawea. Her health, if lack of journal notes means anything, is consistently better than that of any of the men.

Not only rough water but continued rain makes the lives of all the party miserable. On the same day, Friday, November 8, Clark's journal continues:

Some rain all day at intervales, we are all wet and disagreeable, as we have been for Several days past, and our present Situation a verry disagreeable one . . . as we have not leavel land Sufficient for an encampment and for our baggage to lie clear of the tide, the High hills jutting in so close and steep that we cannot retreat back, and the water of the river to Salt to be used, added to this the waves are increasing to such a hight that we cannot move from this place.

Nov. 12   our party has been wet for 8 days and is truly disagreeable, their robes and leather clothes are rotten from being continually wet, and they are not in a situation to get others. fortunately for us our men are healthy.

But how about the nine-months-old baby? Can his mother keep him warm and dry? Nobody knows. Neither of them is mentioned. What concerns the men is the way their canoes are rolled about the beach by the giant waves. They are in danger of being crushed against

those monsterous trees maney of them nearly 200 feet long and from 4 to 7 feet through.

The party is finally compelled to camp on a pile of driftwood, with nothing to eat but dried and pounded fish.

Nov. 14, Thursday 1805 [Clark]   The rain &c which has continued without a longer intermition than 2 hours at a time for ten days past has destroyed the robes and rotted nearly one half of the fiew clothes the party has, particularly the leather clothes fortunately for us we have no very cold weather as yet. and if we have cold weather before we can kill & Dress Skins for clothing the bulk of the party will Suffer verry much. Squar displeased with me for not . . .

He does not complete the statement, but clearly this is a different Sacagawea, who ventures to tell the captain of her displeasure at something he has failed to do.

The men are searching for the bay described by Captain George Vancouver as being near the mouth of the river. Eventually they find it and name it Haley's Bay (later Baker's Bay) for a white man who trades here at intervals. They do not yet find the island also described by Vancouver, though they are able from their camp to scan the whole distance from Pt. Adams to Cape Disappointment.

Before long, they have callers, Chinook Indians, who are all too friendly and soon overrun the camp. These fellows have learned about trading with white men.

Nov. 11 [*Clark*]　*One of these men had on a Salors jacket and Pantaloons and made Signs that he got those clothes from the white people.*

The captains soon learn that the Chinooks will steal anything and everything they see. Sometimes only threats backed up with a show of arms can make them return stolen articles. Writes Clark,

I told them they shoud not come near us and if any of their nation stold anything from us I would have him Shot, which they understood verry well.

Lewis is first to visit the ocean, then Clark decides to go also.

Nov. 17, Sunday [*Clark*]   *I directed all the men who wished to see more of the Ocian to Get ready to set out with me on tomorrow day light. the following men expressed a wish to accompany me, Serj. Nat Pryor, Serjt J. Ordway, Jo. Fields R. Fields Jo. Shannon Jo. Colter, William Bratten, Peter Wiser, Shabono & my servant York, all others being well contented with that Part of the Ocean and its curiosities which could be seen from the vicinity of our Camp.*

Nothing is said about Sacagawea's wanting to go, but later on, her insistence to be included on another trip suggests that she has asked before and been refused. The men are gone several days, and when they return find many Chinook Indians with Captain Lewis. Among them are the one-eyed chief, Comcomly, and his brother, Chil-lar-la-wil. For the first time, the white men see the beautiful fur of sea otters:

November 20 [*Clark*]   *One of the Indians had on a roab made of 2 Sea Otter Skins the fur of them were more butifull than any fur I had ever seen both Capt. Lewis & myself endeavored to purchase the roab with different articles at length we procured it for a belt of blue beeds which the*

118

Squar-Wife of our interpreter Shabono wore around her waste.

Novelists will have a fine time with this incident, supposing that Sacagawea is so in love with Clark that she nobly sacrifices her treasured belt to buy for him the sea otter robe he wants. Nobody can say for sure what happens, but next day Clark writes,

We gave the Squar a coate of Blue Cloth for the belt of Blue Beads we gave for the Sea Otter skins purchased of an Indian.

Is the gift of the blue coat the result of a guilty conscience on the part of the captains? Perhaps, but it is equally possible Sacagawea has not willingly parted with her cherished belt. She may have objected when her husband, at the captains' request, ordered her to surrender the belt. She may make so much fuss they have to do something to pacify her. We do not know; it is merely a guess, but the odds are in its favor.

Terrible weather continues:

Nov. 22 [Clark] Oh how horriable is the day waves braking with great violence against the Shore throwing the water into our camp &c. all wet and confined to our

Shelters . . . we purchased a fiew Wappato roots for which we gave Armbands & rings to the old Squar, those roots are equal to the Irish potato and is a tolerable substitute for bread.

Meanwhile, at the camp of Comcomly, the belt of blue beads has aroused the cupidity of other Indians, and they hasten to the white men's camp with more sea otter skins:

Saturday, November 23 [Clark]   in the evening Seven Indians of the Clat sop Nation came over in a Canoe, they brought with them 2 Sea otter Skins for which they asked blue beads &c. I offered him my Watch, handkerchief a bunch of red beads and a dollar of the American coin, all of which he refused and demanded "ti-a-ce-mo-shack" which is Chief beads *and the most common blue beads, but fiew of which we have at this time.*

The captains must be looking back wistfully to their purchasing days in St. Louis. What beautiful furs they could have bought with a few handfuls of those cheap blue beads!

They decide to move camp to some better place and take a vote on the choice of all those involved, even Janey, as Clark calls Sacagawea. The fact that she claims the right to vote is another indication of her new self-assertiveness. Some of the men want to go back to the falls near The Dalles, but the majority choose the south side of the bay here at the mouth of the Columbia. A trading ship may come in during the winter, from which they can buy supplies. At any rate, the climate is milder here than farther back in the country. There are also more elk, their principal source of food and clothing. Sacagawea's reason for remaining near the coast is that the wappato roots, their one substitute for bread and potatoes, are more plentiful here.

Once more, Clark becomes very ill from the poor diet, but a surprise comes:

November 30 [Clark]   *The squar gave me a piece of bread made of flour which she had reserved for her child and carefully Kept until this time, which has unfortunately got wet and a little Sour. this bread I eate with great satisfaction, it being the only mouthfull I had tasted for several months past.*

Where did Sacagawea get flour to make bread, and when did she bake it? The last time the party has had supplies of flour was in the mountains. Or did she bring it all the way from Fort Mandan? It is probably the hardtack variety of bread so much used by travelers and traders. Little Pomp is nine months old and cutting teeth. He needs something hard to chew on. She probably has carried the hardtack in her *parfleche* all this time, letting no one know of it. She must have recovered from her displeasure with Clark to give him this treasure intended for her baby.

Pryor and Gibson go hunting and are successful in killing six elk. Sacagawea displays another of her culinary tricks:

> *Tuesday, Dec. 5 [Clark]   After eating the marrow out of two shank bones of an Elk, the Squar choped the bones fine boiled them and extracted a pint of Grease, which is Superior to the tallow of the animal . . . I marked my name on a large pine tree . . . William Clark December 3rd 1805. By Land from the U. States in 1804 & 1805.*

The wording of Clark's sign shows that he, as well as Lewis and President Jefferson, has read Alexander MacKenzie's *Voyages.* He has evidently been impressed by the sign MacKenzie painted on a rock to show he had reached the Pacific "by land" and copies the idea.

On this same day, Lewis returns from a scouting trip to report that plenty of elk can be procured near a river which falls into a small bay on the south side of the Columbia. Here his party has brought down six elk and five deer, two of his men remaining behind to guard them.

They are still hampered by the awful weather. Sergeant Gass writes:

There is more wet weather on this coast than I ever knew in
any other place; during a month we have had but three fair
days and there is no prospect of a change.

The men sicken with colds from wearing wet clothes day
and night. Also the Chinook Indians still pester them
demanding blue beads. As Clark says,

Blue beeds is their great trade they are fond of clothes or
blankets of Blue red or brown.

On December 7 the party moves across the river to the place
Lewis has selected. It stands on a rise of ground thirty feet
above high tide, on a stream later to be called the Lewis and
Clark River, which flows into Young's Bay. The two most
immediate needs are shelter and salt with which to preserve
their meat. Trees of which to build huts are here in plenty, but
salt requires setting up a camp near the ocean.

Clark takes five men and journeys overland, reaching the
ocean at the site of future Seaside, Oregon. The stone cairn he
builds will still be intact two hundred years later, as a tourist
attraction. The cairn is a long stove built of round stones the
men have gathered on the beach. It will take logs at least four
feet long which are stuffed in at one end. In the top are five
holes, each large enough to hold a big kettle. The men keep the
fire burning day and night and the kettles full of seawater. As it

evaporates, they scrape the salt from the sides. In this manner they can make three or four quarts of salt per day.

Back at the camp, the rest of the men work at the job of cutting down the huge pine trees and building huts. They have many minor accidents and illnesses. One man dislocates a shoulder, which is so difficult to put back into place that it takes three tries. Another strains a knee, and a third develops boils on his legs.

Having rid themselves of the Chinook Indians, they are now pestered equally by the Clatsops who live on this side of the river. They bring an unwanted gift, fleas, which the white men are unable to remove completely from their robes and blankets. Having run out of blue beads and also white ones, the Indians' second choice, they have trouble buying anything. Sometimes a fishhook will be accepted. The huts go up, to the accompaniment of Indians, fleas, and bad weather.

December 13 [*Clark*]   *We continue our houses of the straightest, and most butifullest logs . . . the timber splits butifully and of any width.*

December 16, Monday   The rain continues, with Tremendous gusts of wind . . . the winds violent, Trees falling in every direction, whorl winds with gusts of rain Hail & Thunder . . . Certainly one of the worst days that ever was!

December 17   Our Leather Lodge has become so rotten that the smallest thing tares it into holes and it is now Scarcely Sufficient to keep off the rain off a Spot Sufficiently large for our bed.

What about the bed where Sacagawea and the baby sleep? Is it also under a dripping hole in the lodge? No mention. What does she do all day long, sitting in the rotten tent under the dripping trees? Very likely what she has always done—cooks, dresses hides, makes moccasins and other clothing, besides caring for her baby. Her work does not seem of enough importance to be mentioned.

By December 20 the men have roofs on four huts. The two captains move in, though their room is unfinished. By Christmas day, all the members of the party have shelters, a cause for celebration as they christen the place Fort Clatsop:

Wednesday, 25th December, 1805 [Clark]   At daylight this morning we were awoke by the discharge of the fire arms of all our party & a Salute, Shouts and a Song which the whole party joined in under our windows, after which they retired to their rooms were cheerful all the morning. After brackfast we divided our Tobacco which amounted to 12 carrots one half of which we gave to the men of the party who used tobacco, and to those who doe not use it we make a present of a handkerchief, The Indians leave us in the evening all the party Snugly fixed in their huts. I received a present of Capt. L. of a fleece hosrie Shirt Draws and Socks, a pair Mockersons of Whitehouse a Small Indian basket of Gutherich [Goodrich], two Dozen white weazil tails of the Indian woman [Sacagawea must have been trapping on her own] & some black root of the Indians before their departure . . .

We would have Spent this day the nativity of Christ in feasting, had we anything either to raise our Sperits or even gratify our appetites, our Diner consisted of pore Elk, so much spoiled that we eate it thro' mear necessity, some Spoiled pounded fish and a fiew roots.

One would like to know what Sacagawea gives her baby for Christmas. He is now almost eleven months old, probably learning to walk. Perhaps she has made him a little shirt, leggings, and moccasins of the soft fur of those weasels whose tails she gives to Clark. Perhaps Pomp spends Christmas playing with the big dog, Scammon, or Clark dances him on his foot, "Trot, Trot to Boston." Or he may take the baby's hands in his own and dance with him about the room. "My little dancing boy," he calls him in a letter written months later.

The men gladly buy wapato roots from the Indians, for a

126

change in diet, "as we are now living on spoiled Elk which is extremely disagreeable to the smel as well as the taste." But a welcome interlude is at hand.

Sunday, 29th December 1805 [Clark]   We were informed day before yesterday that a whale had foundered on the coast . . . and that the greater part of the Clatsops were gorn for the oile & blubber, the wind proves too high for us to proceed by water to See this Monster, Capt. Lewis has been in readiness Since first we heard of the whale to go and see it and collect Some of its Oil, the wind has proved too high as yet for him to proceed.

So the old year goes out on a high wind and a new one is ushered in.

January 1st, Wednesday, 1806 [Lewis]   This morning I was awoke at an early hour by the discharge of a volley of small arms, which were fired by our party in front of our quarters to usher in the new year; this was the only mark of respect which we had it in our power to pay this celebrated day. our repast of this day tho' better than that of Christmas, consisted principally in the anticipation of the 1st day of January, 1807, when in the bosom of our friends we hope to participate in the mirth and hilarity of the day and . . . enjoy the repast which the hand of civilization has prepared for us. at present we were content with eating our boiled Elk and wappetoe, and solacing our thirst with our only beverage, pure water. *two of our hunters who set out this morning returned in the evening having killed two buck elks; they presented Capt. Clark and myself each a marrow bone and tongue, on which we suped.*

Thursday, 2d of January   We are infested with swarms of fleas already in our new habitations; the presumption is therefore strong that we shall not devest ourselves of this intolerably troublesome vermine during our residence here.

Some Indians bring in a sample of whale blubber. When it is cooked, the Americans declare it to be something like pork. Clark decides to journey to the whale and bring home more of this blubber if possible. He sets the date for January 6. How many of the party he plans to take with him, he does not say, but one he does not invite intends to go anyhow. Sacagawea continues to show her new personality.

Monday, 6th of January, 1806 [Clark]   The last evening, Shabono and his Indian woman was very impatient to go with me. [Lewis writes it "importunate"] She observed that She had traveled a long way with us to See the great waters, and that now that monstrous fish was also to be Seen, She thought it very hard that She could not be permitted to See either.

Clark cannot resist the girl's pleas. Perhaps he remembers the belt of blue beads, and the other time they went to the ocean but did not take her. This is to be a great experience for her, one she will remember all her life. She will tell her son how he went to the ocean and saw the whale when he was but a baby on her back.

They go part way by canoe, and on the first night camp near a small river that empties into the bay. The hunters kill an elk which they cook over a fire of driftwood—barbecued elk.

The weather was beautiful, the sky clear, the moon shone brightly, a circumstance the more aggreable as this is the first fair evening we have enjoyed for two months.

This is one of the few references to good weather in all the months they spend at Fort Clatsop.

With a guide they climb Tillamook Head, destined to be a famous landmark on the Oregon coast. On the way, they meet fourteen Indians, both men and women, loaded down with whale oil and blubber. They follow the path down to the beach where the skeleton of the monster lies, already stripped of every valuable part. They bargain earnestly and finally succeed in buying three hundred pounds of blubber and a few gallons of oil. Writes Clark:

Small as this stock is, I prize it highly; and thank providence for directing the whale to us; and think him much more kind to us than he was to jonah, having sent this Monster to be swallowed by us *in Sted of* Swallowing of us *as jonah's did.*

Many years later, this trip of Sacagawea's will become important in assessing opinions about her life. At the moment, however, the journals say nothing of her reactions. One can feel sure that not only the whale impresses her. To a seventeen-year-old girl who has never seen any body of water other than a river or creek, or possibly a small lake, the vast expanse of ocean, with the waves curling in on the beach, must be a spiritual, as well as physical, experience. Never again can life be as small as she has hitherto known it.

In the huts in the forest, all supplies are running low.

Tuesday, January 13, 1806 [Lewis] this evening we exhausted the last of our candles, but fortunately had taken the precaution to bring with us moulds and wick, by means of which and some Elk's tallow in our possession we do not

yet consider ourselves destitute of this necessary article;
the Elk we have killed have a very small portion of tallow.

By this time, all are heartily sick of elk meat, but they have
nothing else except roots and an occasional meal of dog meat.
The Indians show disdain for anyone who eats the latter, their
dogs being the camp scavengers.

The organization of the party has been completed along
military lines. The men are divided into four groups or messes,
the captain's own, and three under command of the sergeants.
Where the Charbonneaus are assigned is not mentioned. Supplies are issued to the sergeants for several days at a time.
Lewis complains of the men's mismanagement of their
rations:

Monday, January 20 1806   on the morning of the eigh-
teenth we issued 6 lbs. of jirked Elk pr. man, this evening the
Sergt. reported that it was all exhausted; the six lbs. have
therefore lasted two days and a half only. at this rate our
seven Elk will last us only 3 days longer, yet no one seems
much concerned about the state of the stores; so much for
habit.

Though as eager as anyone to start home, Lewis knows that
the villain of their drama, the Rocky Mountain barrier, in
winter is buried under twenty feet of snow. It will be June

before even the scantiest subsistence for the horses can be found. He believes two months a sufficient time to reach the foot of the range, so the date of April 1 is set for the probable time of departure. Time hangs heavy on their hands. Over and over the journals report days like this:

Sunday, Feb 2, 1806   Not any occurrence today worthy of notice; but all are pleased that one month of the time which binds us to Fort Clatsop and which separates us from our friends has now elapsed.

Lewis spends much of his time writing up his observations on people, climate, plants, and animals of this region. Clark draws maps of the country through which they have come and plots the return journey. The men of the garrison and, presumably, Sacagawea, are employed in dressing elk skins and making clothing and moccasins. The usual method of tanning is to rub the brains of the animal into the flesh side of the pelt to soften it and make it more pliable. Another favored material for this purpose is soap, composed of grease and lye. These ingredients are not available here. Lewis writes:

they find great difficulty [in preparing the skins] for the want of branes; we have not soap to supply the dificiency, nor can we procure ashes to make the lye; none of the pines which we use for fuel affords any ashes; extrawdinary as it may seem, the greene wood is consoomed without leaving the residium of a particle of ashes.

Food is so short that when someone brings in an elk, it is cause for great rejoicing:

February 8 [Clark]   we have both Dined and suped on Elks tongues and marrowbones, a great Luxury for Fort Clatsop.

Throughout this period of the expedition, illness haunts the party at every turn. Mostly it has been of short duration, but on February 15, the men from the salt cairn come into camp carrying Gibson in a litter. He has had a terrible cold, with high fever, and has become so weak he cannot stand. Lewis gives him diluted nitre, makes him drink plentifully of sage tea and bathe his feet in warm water. At night he administers thirty-five drops of laudanum, which must have given the sick man a full night's sleep.

Within a week, the illness has spread through the camp:

February 22, 1806 [Lewis]   we have not had as many sick at any one time since we left Wood River the general complaint seems to be bad colds and fevers, something I believe of the influenza.

On the 21st of February, the ocean party returns with twenty gallons of salt, twelve of which they store in kegs for the return journey. A small, delicate kind of fish classified as an anchovy begins to run in the rivers. The men dry them over small fires. Sturgeon also become plentiful. Turtle doves and robins, magpies and flycatchers flit among the trees. Spring is coming.

One can imagine Bird Woman taking her baby into the woods to see the wild flowers and birds. The boy is toddling around now, being more than a year old, though he still depends on her abundant milk for most of his food. She spends much time in making clothing and moccasins for the return journey.

The men also have been busy. Clark reports:

Our party are now furnished with 358 pair of Mockersons exclusive of a good portion of Dressed leather, they are also provided with shirts overalls capoes [capotes] of dressed Elk skin for their homeward journey.

Illness and accidents continue to plague the remaining days at Fort Clatsop. Hall suffers a crushed foot and ankle, but luckily no bones are broken. Bratton grows very weak from influenza. None have the sort of food they need.

Sunday, March 2 [Lewis]   The diet of the sick is so inferior that they recover their strength but slowly. none of them are now sick but all in a state of convalescence with keen appetite and nothing to eat except lean Elk meat.

Sunday, March 9   Bratton complains of his back being very painfull to him today; I conceive this pain to be something of the rheumatism.

Tuesday, March 18   Drewyer was taken last night with a violent pain in his side. Capt. Clark blead him. it is truly unfortunate that they should be sick at the moment of our departure.

Yet in all this time, not a word about any illness of Sacagawea or her baby. Their good health seems phenomenal.

Now that they are halfway through March, the men all think eagerly of the time when they can start back up the river. What they need most is new canoes to replace the battered old dugouts in which they came down the Columbia. Then they had the advantage of moving with the current; now they must oppose it.

They look with admiration on the beautiful canoes of the Indians and the skill with which the tribesmen make them, using only the simplest of tools. Foremost among these is a chisel made of an old file, about an inch or inch and a half in width. This is fixed in a block of wood which is held in the right hand and pushed with the left, without the aid of a mallet. Such slow means of working make the men suppose the making of a canoe to be the labor of years, yet they see these Indians make one in a few weeks. They long to buy them. If only that supply ship which the President did not send had come into the bay right now!

The captains are too loyal to their chief to complain, but a certain wistfulness appears in their final notes at Fort Clatsop.

Sunday, March 16, 1806 [Lewis]   *the Indians remained with us all day but would not dispose of their canoes at a price which it was in our power to give consistently with the state of our stock of Merchandise. two handkerchiefs would now contain all the small articles of merchandize which we possess; the ballance of the stock consists of 6 blue robes one scarlet ditto one uniform artillerists' coat and hat, five robes made of our large flag, and a few old cloaths trimmed with ribbon. On this stock we have wholy to depend for the purchase of horses and such portion of our subsistence from the Indians as it will be in our powers to obtain. a scant dependence indeed, for a tour of the distance of that before us.*

Monday, March 17 [Clark]   *Drewyer returned late this evening from the Cath-Iah-mahs with our Indian canoe which Sergt. Pryor had left some days since and also a canoe which he had purchased from those people for this canoe he gave Capt. Lewis's uniform laced coat and nearly half a carrot of tobacco. it seams that nothing except this Coat would induce them to dispose of a canoe which in their mode of traffic is an article of the greatest value except a wife with whome it is nearly equal, and is generally given in exchange to the father for his daughter. I think that the United States are in justice indebted to Capt. Lewis another uniform Coat for that of which he has disposed of on this occasion, it was but little worn.*

One wonders what could have been in Lewis's mind when he chose to bring a uniform dress coat on this sort of trip. Did he expect to return home by sea and perhaps visit some foreign country en route, where he would be presented to the head of state? Apparently it is only dire necessity that makes him part with it now, his loss the more poignant because the coat "was but little worn." Clark continues:

We yet want another canoe as the Clatsops will not sell us one, a proposition has been made by one of our interpts and several of the party to take one in liew of 6 Elk which they stole from us this winter &c.

This is an appealing idea, but evidently they do not put it into practice. Instead, they patch up the boats they have:

Tuesday, March 18 [Lewis]   we directed Sergt. Pryor to prepare the two canoes which Drewyer brought last evening . . . they wanted some knees to strengthen them and several cracks corked and payed. he completed them except the latter operation which the frequent showers in the course of the day prevented as the canoes could not be made sufficiently dry even with the assistance of fire.

Wednesday, March 19   It continued to rain and hail today in such manner that nothing further could be done to the canoes.

Though he had set April 1 as the probable date of departure, Lewis now pushes it ahead a week. He and Clark make out their final reports, leaving one copy in the huts, giving one to Indians to be sent with traders around by sea, and taking one with them. He sums up their experience here:

Thursday, March 20   Altho' we have not fared sumptuously this winter and spring at Fort Clatsop, we have lived quite as comfortably as we had any reason to expect we should and have accomplished every object which induced our remaining at this place except that of meeting with the traders who visit the entrance of this river . . . it would have been very fortunate for us had some of those traders arrived previous to our departure from hence, as we should then have had it in our power to obtain an addition to our stock of merchandize which would have made our homeward bound journey much more comfortable.

The Indians have pushed their advantage too far. Perhaps they thought the white men could not go without more canoes, for which they would pay an extravagant price. Sunday, March 23, arrives, and the white men load the canoes they do have, managing somehow to find a place for everyone and all their remaining goods. In Lewis's words,

at 1 p.m. we bid a final adieu to Fort Clatsop. we had not proceeded more than a mile before we met . . . a party of 20 Chinooks men & women learning that we were in want of a canoe some days past had brought us one for sale, but being already supplyed we did not purchase it.

Sergeant Gass puts the final touch on the story of those days at Clatsop:

From Nov. 4, 1805 to March 25, 1806, not more than 12 days when it did not rain & of these only 6 were clear.

The Indians watch the canoes disappear in the mist. They will remember until they are old men this great moment of their lives. To visitors they will then tell of the white men, the greatest men who ever lived, and of the one Indian woman who came with them.

On the way up the Columbia Lewis makes a side trip to see the Willamette River, which he failed to notice on the down journey. Except for this, the party faithfully retraces its route almost to The Dalles. Here comes the worst insult an Indian could give—to steal Lewis's dog.

Friday, April 11, 1806 [Lewis]   *three of this same tribe of villains the Wah-clel-lars, stole my dog this evening and took him towards their village; I was shortly afterwards informed of this transaction by an indian who spoke the Clatsop language (some of which we had learnt from them during the winter) and sent three men in pursuit of the theives with orders if they made the least resistance or difficulty in surrendering the dog to fire on them; they overtook these fellows or reather came within sight of them at the distance of about 2 miles; the indians discovering the party in pursuit of them left the dog and fled.*

The next day, one canoe gets away when the men are towing it past the rapids and it is lost downstream. They have to re-distribute the crew and cargo among the remaining canoes. Where they place Sacagawea and Pompey, they do not say, but they plan to leave the river soon and go overland.

They approach the part of the country where Sacagawea can understand the language. On Wednesday, April 16, Captain Clark takes the two interpreters, Drewyer and Charbonneau, with Sacagawea, and crosses the river to the south side, just above The Dalles, to trade for horses. Lewis remains in camp and directs his men in making pack saddles for the twelve horses they hope to buy.

For a few days the traders have no luck, except that Charbonneau manages to buy a fine mare for a few ermine tails, elks' teeth, a belt, and some other articles of small value. Are the ermine tails his Christmas present from Sacagawea? Has she also saved the elks' teeth? Who knows?

Clark decides to try a different stratagem to induce the Indians to sell horses. The wife of the chief is very miserable from a lame back. Clark rubs on camphor and applies warm flannels, giving the poor woman much relief. It is easier now to persuade her husband to sell horses. Clark buys two. This is not enough, so the white men prepare to go on in their boats. As the Indians see the source of revenue about to depart, they suddenly relent. Clark buys five more horses for what he calls "emence" prices. At length they have eight horses, but Bratton must be given one of them, since he is still too weak from influenza to walk. Lewis loads the remaining goods on the seven horses. Everybody except Bratton has to go on foot, even Sacagawea, who must also carry Pompey.

Tuesday, April 22, 1806 [Lewis]   we had not arrived at the top of a hill over which the road led opposite the village when Charbono's horse threw his load and taking fright at the saddle and robe which still adhered, ran at full speed down the hill, near the village he disengaged himself from the saddle and robe, an indian hid the robe in his lodge. I sent our guide and one man who was with me in the rear to assist Charbono in retaking his horse which having done they returned to the village . . . in search of lost articles, they found the saddle but could see nothing of the robe the indians denyed having seen it . . . being now confident the indians had taken it I sent the Indian woman on to request Captain Clark to halt the party and send back some of the men . . . being determined either to make the indians deliver the robe or birn their houses.

One of the men finds the robe in an Indian lodge, and the party goes on. They come to the site of the later Arlington, Oregon, marching all day through deep sand and over rocks, suffering greatly from sore feet. The sight of Indians riding good horses, none of which they will sell, drives the travelers frantic. More than once, Lewis must think that if only that supply ship had come, he would have had plenty of goods to tempt the owners of these horses.

At the mouth of the Walla Walla River, they meet Chief Yellept, who had been friendly on the way down the river. He tells them of a shortcut to the Kooskooske River (Clearwater). This road leads up the Walla Walla to the Touchet, then by means of that stream, the Tucannon, and Pataha, finally reaches the Snake River near the later towns of Clarkston, Washington, and Lewiston, Idaho, at the mouth of the Clearwater.

Somewhere along this trail, Sacagawea once more serves as an interpreter:

Monday, April 28, 1806 [Lewis]   We found a Shoshone woman, prisoner among these people by means of whome and Sah-cah-gar-weah we found the means of conversing with the Walla Wallahs, we conversed with them for several hours and fully satisfyed all their enquiries with rispect to ourselves and the objects of our pursuit . . . the fiddle was played and the men amused themselves with dancing about an hour. we then requested the Indians to dance which they very cheerfully complied with; they continued their dance untill 10 at night. the whole assemblage of indians about 550 men women and children sung and danced at the same time . . . they were much gratifyed with seeing some of our party join them in their dance.

For more than a week we hear nothing further about Sacagawea. By May 8, the party has proceeded up the Clearwater River far enough to meet the Nez Percé Indians and Chief Twisted Hair, with whom they had left their horses for the winter.

This chief, who had been kind to the starving white men in the fall, has also proved his friendship by taking good care of their horses. The animals are now out on the open range, and he sends men to bring them in.

The white men spend a week or two in the Nez Percé camp, waiting for the snow in the mountains to melt enough so they can find the trail used by this tribe on their annual excursions to the buffalo country.

Chief Twisted Hair's sister has a small son, Tamootsin, about six years old. As later events will prove, he forms a great attachment for the white captains, particularly Clark. While his mother visits with Sacagawea and plays with Pompey, the little boy probably hangs around watching the white men repair their equipment. Clark, who is always fond of children, pays attention to him and wins the boy's admiration.

This friendship will have great importance in times to

come. Thirty years later, when Tamootsin is in his middle thirties, the missionary Henry Harmon Spalding, companion of Dr. Marcus Whitman, will come to this part of Idaho. He will establish his home and mission school at Lapwai, a few miles up the Clearwater from its confluence with the Snake River. Here Tamootsin will become one of his first two converts and will be baptized with the Christian name of Timothy. Baptized with him will be his wife's father, Old Chief Joseph, so called to distinguish him from his famous son, Chief Joseph of the Nez Percé.

Timothy's services to the white men will be many and varied, but all will stem from the fact that the red-headed white chief who loves children takes time to be kind to the little Indian boy.

The white hunters bring in a deer which they share with the Nez Percés. Among the crowd is a young Shoshone brave. Lewis desires Sacagawea to talk with him, but the man is sulky. Clark reports:

The Snake Indian was much displeased that he was not furnished with as much Deer as he could eate. he refused to speak to the wife of Shabono, through whome we could understand the natives. we did not indulge him and in the after part of the day he came too and spoke very well.

Next morning the party starts on, but falling snow makes travel slippery and difficult. They pass a village where Lewis says,

The noise of their women pounding kouse roots reminds me of a nail factory.

The Indians, including the young Snake, follow along, and again Sacagawea and her husband talk with the boy, "altho it had to pass through French, Minnetaree, Shoshone and Chopunnish."

Many of the Nez Percé are sick. Lewis diagnoses scrofula, ulcers, rheumatism, sore eyes, and weakness of the legs. He mixes quantities of "eye water" and treats forty or fifty applicants every morning.

Sacagawea is back in the country she knows. With joy she observes the plants she has used since childhood.

Friday, May 16 [Lewis] Sahcargarweah gathered a quantity of the roots of a species of fennel which we found very agreeable food, the flavor of this root is not unlike annis seed, and they dispel the wind which the roots called Cows [kouse] and quamash [camas] are apt to create particularly the latter. We also boil a small onion which we find in great abundance . . . the mush of roots we find adds much to the comfort of our diet.

Sunday, May 18 [Lewis]   Our Indian woman was busily engaged today in laying in a store of the fennel roots for the Rocky Mountains.

The men have run into the same trouble with camas as before. Lewis says:

This root is pallateable but disagrees with me in every shape I have ever used it.

Scammon resumes his favorite way of hunting:

Friday, May 23 [Lewis]   Sergt. Pryor wounded a deer early this morning in a lick near camp; my dog pursued it into the river; the two young Indian men who had remained with us all night mounted their horses swam the river and drove the deer into the water again; Sergt. Pryor killed it as it reached the shore on this side.

Ever since his birth, Pompey has enjoyed good health, but suddenly he becomes very ill, and the whole camp is upset.

Thursday, May 22 [Lewis]   Charbono's child is very ill this evening; he is cutting teeth and for several days past has had a violent lax [diarrhea] which having suddenly stoped he was attacked with a high fever and his neck and throat are much swolen this evening. we gave him a doze of creem of tartar and flour of sulpher and applyed a poltice of boiled onions to his neck as warm as he could well bear it.

Friday, May 23   he is considerably better this morning tho' the swelling of the neck has abated but little; we still apply poltices of onions which we renew frequently in the course of the day and night.

Saturday, May 24   The child was very wrestless last night [the first time they have remarked on his keeping them awake] it's jaw and the back of it's neck are much more swolen than they were yesterday tho' his fever has abated considerably.

Sunday, May 25   the child is more unwell than yesterday.

Monday, May 26   it is clear of fever this evening and much better, the swelling is considerably abated and appears as if it would pass off without coming to a head, we still continue fresh poltices of onions to the swolen part.

Tuesday, May 27   Charbono's son is much better today, tho' the swelling on the side of his neck I believe will terminate in an ugly imposthume [abscess] a little below the ear.

Wednesday, May 28   The Child is better, he is free of fever, the imposthume is not so large but seems to be advancing to maturity.

Some of the men are apparently moving camp and get into trouble:

Friday, May 30 [Gass]   *Two of our men in a canoe attempting to swim their horses over the river, struck the canoe against a tree and she immediately sank; but they got on shore with the loss of 3 blankets a blanket-coat etc. There are only 3 men in the party who have more than a blanket apiece.*

One blanket is not much cover during the cold mountain nights, so everyone must be eager to complete the crossing of the Bitterroots, delayed by the depth of snow still present. During this wait, much attention has been given to the baby, who now seems almost well.

Tuesday, June 3   the child is nearly well; the imposthume on his neck has in a great measure subsided and left a hard lump underneath his left ear; we still continue the application of the onion poltices.

Thursday, June 5 [Clark]   *the child is recovering fast the inflammation has subsided intirely, we discontinued the poltice, and applyed a plaster of basilicon; the part is still considerably swolen and hard.* [Lewis] *I applied a plaster of sarve* [salve] *made of the rozen of the long leafed pine, Beaswax and Bears oil mixed, which has subsided the inflomation entirely, the part is considerably swelled and hard.*

Sunday, June 8   the child is nearly well.

With obvious relief the two captains end the running account of the baby's illness. While he has been sick, little else has been recorded. When they no longer mention him in their daily notes, it is a sign of their relaxation.

Not once in the two weeks has either of them mentioned the child's mother. One might almost think she is not there, but we know this is not so. The failure to mention her is only one more indication of the light regard in which she is held except when performing some service for them.

One knows without being told that it is she who digs the onions, boils them, and prepares the poultices, once the captains have shown her how. It is she who sits on the ground beside his bed, who rocks him back and forth when he is restless, who holds him to her comforting breast, and who watches day and night with the anxiety of mothers everywhere when their children are ill. She deserves better of the captains than the indifference they show toward her.

Lewis decides that they will now attempt the crossing of the mountains. Perhaps because the little boy of whom all have become fond is once more well, but also because they feel they are really going home, the men cannot contain their high spirits.

Monday, June 9 [Lewis]   our party seems much elated with the idea of moving on towards their friends and country, they all seem allirt in their movements today; they have everything in readiness for a move and notwithstanding the want of provision have been amusing themselves very merrily today in runing footraces, pitching quites prison basse etc.

[Clark]   The flat head river is still falling fast and is nearly as low as it was at the time we arrived this place. this fall of water is what the nativs have informed us was a proper token for us. When the river fell the snows would be sufficiently melted for us to cross the mountains.

They set out the next day, June 10. The hills are covered with the blue flowers of the camas, whose roots the Indians use for bread. This is the root that has twice made all the white men sick, yet the flower is so beautiful that Lewis has to write of it:

From the color of its bloom at a short distance it resembles lakes of fine clear water, so complete is this deseption that on first sight I could have swoarn it was water.

151

Again they have to wait because of deep snow, so it is June 30 when they reach Travellers Rest creek. Here the party divides. Lewis takes a small party to try out the more direct route to the falls of the Missouri which the Indians described to him the fall before. There he will leave Thompson, McNeal, and Goodrich to prepare their wheels and carriers to take the canoes back over the portage.

With six volunteers he himself will ascend the Marias River to see where it comes from. President Jefferson had hoped that some river from the north could provide a waterway from the Athabasca and thus set up a new trade route.

Clark and the rest of the party will go to the head of the Jefferson River and recover the canoes sunk there last fall. Sergeant Ordway with nine men will then take them down to the falls of the Missouri. Captain Clark and the rest of the party, including Charbonneau, Sacagawea, and York, will go overland to the Yellowstone River, make canoes, and float down to the Missouri. Sergeant Pryor and two men are detailed to conduct the horses overland to the Mandan country. Not all these plans will work out, but they are made.

On July 3 the two parties start. For a while, Pryor and his fifty horses accompany Clark's party. On the Fourth, they celebrate with a big dinner of venison and the root "mush" Sacagawea concocts. Clark is not sure of the route back to the place where the canoes were sunk in the river and some goods cached. This is one of the few times when Sacagawea can be said to be his guide:

Sunday, 6th July [Clark]   The Indian woman wife to Shabono informed me that she had been in this plain frequently and knew it well that the creek which we descended was a branch of Wisdom river and when we assended the higher part of the plain we would discover a gap in the mountains in our direction to the canoes, and when we arived at that gap we would see a high point of a mountain covered with snow in our direction to the canoes. We proceeded on 1 mile and Crossed a larger Creek from the right which heads in a snow Mountain and Fish Creek over which there was a road through a gap [Big Hole Pass]. we assended a small rise and beheld an open butifull Leavel Vally or plain of about 20 [15] miles wide and near 60 [30] long extending N.&S. in every direction around which I could see high points of Mountains covered with snow. I discovered one at a distance very high covered with snow which bore S.80°E. The Squar pointed to the gap through which she said we must pass which was S.56°E. She said we would pass the river before we reached the gap. [Near their night camp will be fought the Battle of Big Hole, August 9, 1877, when Indians under Chief Joseph will escape.]

Sacagawea's directions prove correct. The expedition follows the south fork of Wisdom River, crosses several tributaries, and comes to the Divide between the Wisdom (Big Hole) and Jefferson (Beaverhead) Rivers, near the site of a later town, Bannock, Montana. Here they find their sunken canoes and the supplies they cached in the fall, including some tobacco. The men who have been deprived of this luxury for months almost go mad:

> *Tuesday, July 8 [Clark]   the most of the Party with me being chewers of Tobacco become so impatient to be chewing it that they scarcely gave themselves time to take their saddles off their horses before they were off to the deposit.*

Everything is safe except one canoe which has a big hole in it. They raise, clean, and repair the others and load them to go down the Jefferson and Missouri rivers to meet Lewis and his party. Sacagawea again calls to mind something of her past:

> *Wednesday, July 9   the Squar brought me a Plant the root of which the nativs eat. this root resembles a carrot in form and Size and something of its colour, being of a pailer yellow than that of our carrot, the Stem and leaf is much like the common carrot and the taste not unlike.*

The party moves rapidly. On July 13 they reach Three Forks of the Missouri and again divide. Some start with the canoes, while Clark and his reduced party move overland toward the Yellowstone. Pryor and the horses, now forty-nine in number, accompany them for a while. They camp on the Gallatin River, where Clark writes:

> *I observe Several leading roads which appear to pass to a gap of the mountains in a E.N.E. direction about 18 or 20 miles distant. The Indian woman who has been of great service to me as a pilot through this country recommends a gap in the mountains more south which I shall cross [Bozeman Pass].*

This compliment paid by Clark to Sacagawea is undoubtedly the source of the legend which attributes to her the title of "guide." From it some will infer that she has performed this service throughout the trip. Quite obviously her guiding has been limited to this special area in the mountains which she remembers from childhood. It is useful to Clark, but since he sees the gap himself, he would have no trouble finding his own way there without her help. He merely wants to be nice to her and express his thanks for the last few days' work.

On the Gallatin River they find several canoes left here the fall before. They are no longer seaworthy, so the men remove the nails, which are too valuable to be left behind, and use the boards to make pack saddles. Beaver swarm here, and the whole valley is swampy.

Relieved of the constraint of Lewis's presence and basking in Clark's favor, Sacagawea becomes more relaxed and talkative.

Monday, July 14 [Clark]   here the squar informed me that there was a large road passing through the upper part of this low plain from Madicins River through the gap I was steering my course to . . . I saw Elk, deer & Antelopes, and a great deal of old signs of buffalow, their roads is in every direction. The Indian woman informs me that a fiew years ago Buffalow was very plenty in those plains & Vallies quite as high as the head of Jeffersons river, but fiew of them ever come into those Vallys of late years owing to the Shoshones who are fearfull of passing into the plains . . . Small parties of Shoshones do pass over to the plains for a few days at a time and kill buffalo for their skins and dried meat, and return imediately into the mountains.

Perhaps Sacagawea has been hoping to see her people here. She may think that by this time they will have forgiven her for siding with the white men last fall. Perhaps she even hopes to take her sister's little boy with her to the Mandan country. She is disappointed, as they do not meet any of her tribe. Very likely they are still at their summer camp on the Lemhi River.

This overland journey is very hard on the horses. Their hoofs become worn down to the quick so they can hardly step. Clark has the men make moccasins of green buffalo skin for the animals, a tactic which seems to relieve them.

A new problem presents itself. They can find no trees large enough for canoes in which to float down the Yellowstone River. While searching for trees, they see a rude fort built of logs and bark.

the Squaw informs me that when the war parties (of Min-nitarees, Crows &c who fight Shoshones) find themselves pursued they make these forts to defend themselves in from the pursuers whose superior numbers might otherwise overpower them.

The fort appears to have been built only a short time ago. Sacagawea may well wonder if her brother could have been here and whether any of her people were killed.

Still failing to find trees big enough for the usual canoe size Clark decides to make two smaller ones and lash them together. They will be twenty-eight feet long, sixteen or eighteen inches deep and sixteen to twenty-four inches wide. One night, while they are engaged in this work, half their horses disappear. For days they try to find them, then conclude that Indians stole them. On another night, either wolves or Indian dogs raid their supplies of dried meat, placed high on a scaffold. They decide to leave this territory.

Clark now carries out the plan of sending Pryor, Gibson, Shannon, and Windsor overland with the remaining horses. They represent bargaining money with which they can buy supplies. He himself and the remaining members of his party load their baggage into the canoes, which have been lashed together for greater stability. In this rather frail craft they set sail on the great, turbulent Yellowstone. A few days later comes a moment that will forever mark this part of their trail:

Friday 25th July at 4 P.M. arrived at a remarkable rock situated in an extensive bottom on the Starboard Side of the river & 250 paces from it . . . This rock which I shall call Pompey's Tower [later to be called Pompey's Pillar] is 200 feet high and 400 paces in secumpherance . . . The nativs have ingraved on the face of this rock the figures of animals &c near which I marked my name and the day of the month & year.

Thus does Clark pay tribute to his affection for the little boy who so recently was desperately ill. If Sacagawea knew how to write, she would put this down as one of the high moments of the trip. Little does she, or Clark either, guess that more than two hundred years later the name on the rock will be protected by an iron grating and that tourists will go out of their way to see it and so remember her child and the white man's love for him.

One of the worst trials of this part of the trip is the prevalence of mosquitoes. They make life almost unbearable. The men cannot work or hunt. Poor little Pomp is so badly bitten that his cheeks are all puffed up. Sleep is impossible. Mosquitoes are so thick on the barrels of the rifles that no one can take aim. The only possible relief is to go to a sandbar in the middle of the river where, if the wind is blowing, the insects do not come.

At this same time, far up north on the Marias River, Lewis experiences the same discomfort.

July 11 [*Lewis*] *We are now troubled with another enemy, not quite so dangerous* [*as the Blackfeet Indians*] *though even more disagreeable. these are the mosquitoes who now infest us in such myriads that we frequently get them into our throats when breathing and the dog even howls with the torture they occasion.*

On Tuesday, August 3, Clark and his party arrive at the confluence of the Yellowstone and Missouri rivers, where they have planned to meet Captain Lewis. Here also the mosquitoes are unendurable.

Wednesday, August 4, 1806 [Clark]   The torments of those musquetors and the want of a Sufficiency of Buffalow meat to dry, those animals not to be found in this neighborhood induce me to . . . proceed on to a more eliagiable Spot on the Missouri below . . . wrote a note to Captain Lewis informing him of my intentions and tied it to a pole which I had stuck up in the point . . . The child of Shabono has been so much bitten by the Musquetors that his face is much puffed up and Swelled.

On August 8, to Clark's great surprise, Pryor and his three companions appear, floating down the Yellowstone in two bull-boats. All the rest of the horses having been stolen, he has no further reason to go overland to the Mandan country, so joins the party at the mouth of the Yellowstone. Even in the misery of mosquitoes, Sacagawea finds eatable food.

Monday 9th August 1806 [Clark]   The Squaw brought me a large and well flavoured Gooseberry of a rich crimson colour and a deep purple berry of the large Cherry of the Current Species . . . the Indian Current.

Thursday 12th August   at Meridian Capt. Lewis hove

in sight with the party which went by way of the Missouri as well as that which accompanied him from Travellers Rest on Clarks River.

So ends what has probably been for Sacagawea the happiest weeks of her life, traveling with Clark who adores her little son and makes her feel so free and easy she can talk and act naturally.

The entire party is now reunited. In a few quick days of floating down the Missouri they reach their starting place, the Mandan villages.

Saturday 17th of August 1806 [Clark]   Settled with Touisant Chabono for his services as an enterpreter the price of a horse and lodge purchased of him for public Service in all amounting to 500$ 33⅓ cents. derected two of the largest of the Canoes be fastened together with poles tied across them So as to make them Study for the purpose of conveying the Indians and enterpreter and their families . . . we also took our leave of T. Chabono, his Snake Indian wife and their son who had accompanied us on our route to the pacific ocean in the capacity of interpreter and interpretess. T. Chabono wished much to accompany us in the said Capacity if we could have prevailed upon the Menetaree Chiefs to decend the river with us to the

U. States, but as none of those Chiefs of whose language he was Conversant would accompany us, his services were no longer of use to the U. States and he was therefore discharged and paid up. we offered to convey him down to the Illinois if he chose to go, he declined proceeding on at present, observing that he had no acquaintance or prospects of makeing a living below, and must continue to live in the way he had done. I offered to take his little son a butifull promising child who is 19 months old to which both himself & wife were willing provided the child had been weaned. they observed that in one year the boy would be sufficiently old to leave his mother & he would then take him to me if I would be so freindly as to raise the child for him in such a manner as I thought proper, to which I agreed &c.

Clark hands over to Charbonneau the $533.33⅓ in cash. How the extra $33 came into the picture is not stated. Sacagawea, being only a squaw, receives nothing. Perhaps Clark lifts up little Pomp for a good-by hug. He may pat Sacagawea's shoulder. Perhaps he shakes hands with Charbonneau. He may wonder whether this white man who has experienced life among his own kind for seventeen months can be contented to go back to the squaw-man existence he lived before.

And what of Sacagawea? What is in her mind? Clark may think she is willing to let him take her baby, but later she will tell her friend Earth Woman that when she hears him make the offer, she wants to hold her child close in her arms. Yet she knows that her husband has the final say. If he agrees, she will have to let the child go. She must be greatly relieved when he decides they must wait a year.

As for herself, does she know that she can never again enter fully into the simple, unquestioning life of an Indian woman? That having tasted respect and consideration, she can never again willingly accept slavery?

One can only guess. One thing is certain: She does not know she has been the heroine in a world drama which has made more secure to the United States all the country west of the Rocky Mountains.

The play is over, its ending something of an anticlimax. The two heroes move on to new parts; the heroine fades into the background, leaving little trace. For one hundred years no one will be sufficiently curious about her even to ask what becomes of her afterward. Only because of a chance occurrence, at this time unimaginable, will anyone ever ask.

Then the day will come when once more she will be the heroine, honored all over the country, especially the part of it she helped to save to the United States. Parks, lakes, and schools, bridges, hotels, and motels will be named for her; statues will be erected to her; books, poems, and operas will tell her story; at least two locations will claim to be her last resting place.

But on this seventeenth day of August, 1806, neither she nor anyone else can guess that this is to happen. Once more the humble, obedient Indian wife, she takes her little boy by the hand, steps out of the canoe, out of history, and back into legend.

AFTERWARD

SACAGAWEA'S ROLE IN HISTORY IS FINISHED, her contribution made. There is no record that Lewis or Clark or any of their crew pay any further attention to her or think much about what happens to her. So faint is the trail she leaves, it is as hard to follow as that of a child lost in the forest. A light footprint here, a strand of dark hair there, the chance meeting with a stranger who reports having seen her, a few words in a journal—these are all an inquirer has to go on.

Mostly, one tries to follow her by tracing the activities of her husband and son. In April 1811, Charbonneau begins what is probably the best job he has ever had, except for the journey with Lewis and Clark. He lands a place with foremost trader of the Missouri, Manuel Lisa.

Lisa is a man of tremendous energy and skill who has been established in the fur trade for over half of his forty years. In

1807, only one year after the Lewis and Clark expedition, he went up the river to the Yellowstone and ascended that stream to the mouth of the Bighorn, where he built his first trading post.

On May 8, 1812, Manuel Lisa loads two boats with merchandise, assembles a party of eighty-seven men, and starts up the river. He plans to establish a place for permanent residence and chooses a site near the border of the modern North and South Dakota. Here his men begin felling trees and building a fort. The traders, among them Toussaint Charbonneau, range the country as far as two hundred miles in every direction for the furs which are immediately shipped to St. Louis.

Lisa's head clerk is John C. Luttig, who keeps a journal of daily happenings. He records the celebration on Thursday, November 19 when the fort is finally finished and on Sunday, December 20, Luttig reports:

"This evening the wife of Charbonneau a Snake squaw died of a putrid fever. She was a good and the best Woman in the fort, aged about 25 years she left a fine infant girl."

Years later, in 1825, a list of the members of the expedition is shown to William Clark, with the request that he write after each name what has happened to that person. After Sacagawea's name he writes "Dead," although he does not mention when she died or who told him about it.

Even though Sacagawea may have lived but a short life and

died without much notice, there can be no doubt as to the importance of her contribution to the Lewis and Clark expedition. Without her efforts the expedition might have failed and thus hampered, perhaps permanently, the expansion of America to the Pacific. This courageous young Shoshone woman has secured a place in the history of this country that is just as firm as that of Lewis and Clark themselves.

BIBLIOGRAPHY

QUOTATIONS FROM THE JOURNALS OF LEWIS AND Clark used in this book are taken from the Thwaites edition unless another source is indicated by name in parentheses, as (Biddle). Usually authorship is indicated by name in brackets, as [Lewis] or [Clark]. Quotations from other journals are identified as [Ordway], [Gass], etc.

Books and articles used in preparing the manuscript were:

DE VOTO, BERNARD, editor, *The Journals of Lewis and Clark.* Boston: Houghton Mifflin Company, 1953.

FRÉMONT, JOHN C., *Report of the Exploring Expedition to the Rocky Mountains.* Washington, D.C., 1845, pp. 30–31.

GASS, PATRICK, *Journal of the Lewis and Clark Expedition.* Indexed by James Kendall Hosmer, LLD. Chicago, A. C. McClurg & Co., 1904.

JACKSON, DONALD, editor, *Letters of the Lewis and Clark Expedition with Related Documents,* 1783–1854. Urbana, University of Illinois Press, 1962.

JOSEPHY, ALVIN M. JR., *The Nez Perce Indians and the Opening of the Northwest.* New Haven and London, Yale University Press, 1965.

LEWIS, MERIWETHER, *The Lewis and Clark Expedition,* 1814 Edition, Unabridged (Biddle Edition), 3 vols. Philadelphia and New York, J. B. Lippincott Company, 1961.

LUTTIG, JOHN C., *Journal of a Fur-Trading Expedition on the Upper Missouri,* 1812–1813, edited by Stella M. Drumm. St. Louis, Missouri State Historical Society, 1920.

ORDWAY, JOHN, *Journal.* In collection of Wisconsin State Historical Society, 1902–1918.

THWAITES, REUBEN GOLD, *Original Journals of the Lewis and Clark Expedition,* 1804–1806. New York: Dodd, Mead & Company, 1904.

TOMKINS, CALVIN, *The Lewis and Clark Trail.* New York, Harper & Row, 1965.

VESTAL, STANLEY, *The Missouri.* New York and Toronto, Farrar & Rinehart, Inc., 1945.

WHITEHOUSE, JOSEPH, *Journal of the Lewis & Clark Expedition.* Included in REUBEN GOLD THWAITES, *Original Journals of the Lewis and Clark Expedition,* 1804–1806. New York, Dodd, Mead & Company, 1904.

Index

ABOUT THE AUTHOR

Neta Lohnes Frazier was born in Michigan and moved west with her family to Spokane, Washington, when she was fifteen. After graduating from Whitman College she taught school where she met her husband, a fellow teacher. A few years later they moved to a farm a few miles from Spokane where she kept busy with an apple orchard, a huge garden, and a very bossy cow.

She turned to writing books for young people using the West as background. Mrs. Frazier is the author of fourteen books for young readers including four that were Junior Literary Guild selections. Her books were well researched and most were based on Pacific Northwest history.

Neta Lohnes Frazier died at the age of 100 in Waitsburg, Washington.

BOOKS IN THIS SERIES

✹STERLING POINT BOOKS